Qualifications and Credit Framework (QCF)
LEVEL 3 DIPLOMA IN ACCOUNTING

(QCF)

QUESTION BANK

Costs and Revenues

2012 Edition

First edition 2010
Third edition July 2012

ISBN 9781 4453 9489 3
(Previous ISBN 9780 7517 9762 6)

British Library Cataloguing-in-Publication Data
A catalogue record for this book is available from the British Library

Published by

BPP Learning Media Ltd
BPP House
Aldine Place
London W12 8AA

www.bpp.com/learningmedia

Printed in the United Kingdom

CONTENTS

Introduction v

Question and answer bank

Chapter tasks	Questions	Answers
1 Introduction to cost accounting	3	51
2 Cost classification and cost behaviour	6	53
3 Material costs and inventory valuation	11	56
4 Labour costs and expenses	15	59
5 Accounting for overheads	19	62
6 Absorption costing	22	64
7 Costing systems I	27	66
8 Costing systems II	30	69
9 Budgeting: fixed and flexed budgets	33	72
10 Variance analysis	36	75
11 Cost bookkeeping	38	76
12 Marginal costing	40	77
13 Short-term decision making	42	79
14 Long-term decision making	46	82
AAT practice assessment 1	87	101
AAT practice assessment 2	111	127
BPP practice assessment 1	139	153
BPP practice assessment 2	163	177
BPP practice assessment 3	185	199
BPP practice assessment 4	207	221
BPP practice assessment 5	233	249
BPP practice assessment 6	261	277

A NOTE ABOUT COPYRIGHT

Dear Customer

What does the little © mean and why does it matter?

Your market-leading BPP books, course materials and e-learning materials do not write and update themselves. People write them: on their own behalf or as employees of an organisation that invests in this activity. Copyright law protects their livelihoods. It does so by creating rights over the use of the content.

Breach of copyright is a form of theft – as well as being a criminal offence in some jurisdictions, it is potentially a serious breach of professional ethics.

With current technology, things might seem a bit hazy but, basically, without the express permission of BPP Learning Media:

- Photocopying our materials is a breach of copyright

- Scanning, ripcasting or conversion of our digital materials into different file formats, uploading them to facebook or emailing them to your friends is a breach of copyright

You can, of course, sell your books, in the form in which you have bought them – once you have finished with them. (Is this fair to your fellow students? We update for a reason.)

And what about outside the UK? BPP Learning Media strives to make our materials available at prices students can afford by local printing arrangements, pricing policies and partnerships which are clearly listed on our website. A tiny minority ignore this and indulge in criminal activity by illegally photocopying our material or supporting organisations that do. If they act illegally and unethically in one area, can you really trust them?

INTRODUCTION

This is BPP Learning Media's AAT Question Bank for Costs and Revenues. It is part of a suite of ground breaking resources produced by BPP Learning Media for the AAT's assessments under the qualification and credit framework.

The Costs and Revenues assessment will be **computer assessed**. As well as being available in the traditional paper format, this **Question Bank is available in an online environment** containing tasks similar to those you will encounter in the AAT's testing environment. BPP Learning Media believe that the best way to practise for an online assessment is in an online environment. However, if you are unable to practise in the online environment you will find that all tasks in the paper Question Bank have been written in a style that is as close as possible to the style that you will be presented with in your online assessment.

This Question Bank has been written in conjunction with the BPP Text, and has been carefully designed to enable students to practise all of the learning outcomes and assessment criteria for the units that make up Costs and Revenues. It is fully up to date as at June 2012 and reflects both the AAT's unit guide and the practice assessment(s) provided by the AAT.

This Question Bank contains these key features:

- tasks corresponding to each chapter of the Text. Some tasks are designed for learning purposes, others are of assessment standard

- the AAT's practice assessment(s) and answers for Costs and Revenues and further BPP practice assessments

The emphasis in all tasks and assessments is on the practical application of the skills acquired.

VAT

You may find tasks throughout this Question Bank that need you to calculate or be aware of a rate of VAT. This is stated at 20% in these examples and questions.

BPP LEARNING MEDIA

Approaching the assessment

When you sit the assessment it is very important that you follow the on screen instructions. This means you need to carefully read the instructions, both on the introduction screens and during specific tasks.

When you access the assessment you should be presented with an introductory screen with information similar to that shown below (taken from the introductory screen from one of the AAT's practice assessments for Costs and Revenues).

This assessment is in TWO sections.
You must show competence in BOTH sections.
You should therefore attempt and aim to complete EVERY task in EACH section.
Each task is independent. You will not need to refer to your answers to previous tasks.
Read every task carefully to make sure you understand what is required.

Where the date is relevant, it is given in the task data.
Both minus signs and brackets can be used to indicate negative numbers UNLESS task instructions say otherwise.

You must use a full stop to indicate a decimal point.
For example, write 100.57 NOT 100,57 or 100 57

You may use a comma to indicate a number in the thousands, but you don't have to.
For example, 10000 and 10,000 are both OK.

Other indicators are not compatible with the computer-marked system.

Section 1   Complete all 5 tasks

Section 2   Complete all 5 tasks

The actual instructions will vary depending on the subject you are studying for. It is very important you read the instructions on the introductory screen and apply them in the assessment. You don't want to lose marks when you know the correct answer just because you have not entered it in the right format.

In general, the rules set out in the AAT practice assessments for the subject you are studying for will apply in the real assessment, but you should read the information carefully on this screen again in the real assessment, just to make sure. This screen may also confirm the VAT rate used if applicable.

A full stop is needed to indicate a decimal point. We would recommend using minus signs to indicate negative numbers and leaving out the comma signs to indicate thousands, as this results in a lower number of key strokes and less margin for error when working under time pressure. Having said that, you can use whatever is easiest for you as long as you operate within the rules set out for your particular assessment.

You have to show competence in both sections of assessments and you should therefore complete all of the tasks. Don't leave questions unanswered.

In some assessments written or complex tasks may be human marked. In this case you are given a blank space or table to enter your answer into. You are told in the practice assessments which tasks these are (note: there may be none if all answers are marked by the computer).

If these involve calculations, it is a good idea to decide in advance how you are going to lay out your answers to such tasks by practising answering them on a word document, and certainly you should try all such tasks in this question bank and in the AAT's environment using the practice assessments.

When asked to fill in tables, or gaps, never leave any unanswered blanks, even if you are unsure of the answer. Fill in your best estimate.

Note that for some assessments where there is a lot of scenario information or tables of data provided (eg tax tables), you may need to access these via 'pop-ups'. Instructions will be provided on how you can bring up the necessary data during the assessment.

Finally, take note of any task specific instructions once you are in the assessment. For example, you may be asked to enter a date in a certain format or to enter a number to a certain number of decimal places.

Remember you can practise the BPP questions in this Question Bank in an online environment on our dedicated AAT Online page. On the same page is a link to the current AAT Practice Assessments as well.

If you have any comments about this book, please e-mail paulsutcliffe@bpp.com or write to Paul Sutcliffe, Senior Publishing Manager, BPP Learning Media Ltd, BPP House, Aldine Place, London W12 8AA.

Question bank

Costs and Revenues Question bank

Chapter 1

Task 1.1

Drag and drop the correct answers into the table below:

1. Annual
2. When required
3. External to the organisation
4. Historic
5. Internal management
6. Specified by law
7. To be useful
8. Historic and future

	Financial accounting	Management accounting
Users		
Timing		
Type of information		
Format		

Task 1.2

Drag and drop the correct answers into the table below:

1. Prime cost
2. Materials
3. Production overheads
4. Production cost
5. Non-production overheads
6. Total cost

```
┌─────────────────────────────────────────────┐
│  COST CARD                                    │
│                                        £      │
│                                               │
│  Direct  [_____]                  X      │
│  Direct labour                         X      │
│  Direct expenses                       X̲      │
│  [_____]                          X      │
│  [_____]                          X̲      │
│  [_____]                          X      │
│  [_____]                            │
│      –  selling and distribution       X      │
│      –  administration                 X      │
│      –  finance                        X̲      │
│  [_____]                          X̲      │
└─────────────────────────────────────────────┘
```

Task 1.3

Which of the following would be classed as indirect labour?

☐ A coach driver in a transport company

☐ Machine operators in a milk bottling plant

☐ A maintenance assistant in a factory maintenance department

☐ Plumbers in a construction company

Task 1.4

For which of the following is a profit centre manager normally responsible?

☐ Cost only

☐ Costs and revenues

☐ Costs, revenues and investment

Task 1.5

Which of the following items would be treated as an indirect cost?

☐ Wood used to make a chair

☐ Metal used for the legs of a chair

☐ Fabric to cover the seat of a chair

☐ Staples to fix the fabric to the seat of a chair

Task 1.6

Prime cost is:

☐ All costs incurred in manufacturing a product

☐ The total of direct costs

☐ The material cost of a product

☐ The cost of operating a department

Chapter 2

Task 2.1

Drag and drop the correct entries into the table below, based on whether each one would be classified as a production cost, a selling and distribution cost or an administration cost:

(a) Factory heat and light
(b) Finance Director's salary
(c) Sales Director's salary
(d) Depreciation of delivery vans
(e) Depreciation of plant and machinery
(f) Fuel and oil for delivery vans

	Drag and drop choice
Production cost	
Selling and distribution cost	
Administration cost	

Task 2.2

Look at the two graphs below. **What costs do they depict?**

Graph A

☐ variable cost per unit

☐ fixed cost per unit

☐ total fixed cost across level of activity

☐ total variable cost

Graph B

☐ a variable cost per unit

☐ fixed cost per unit

☐ total fixed cost across level of activity

☐ total variable cost

Graph A

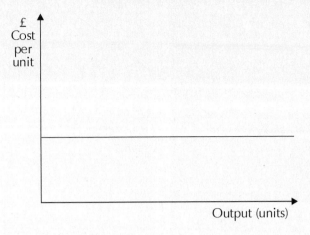

Graph B

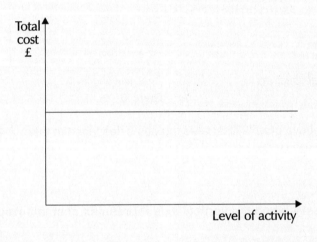

Task 2.3

Calculate the fixed and variable elements of the following costs using the high-low technique:

Month	Output (units)	Total cost £
January	16,000	252,500
February	18,500	290,000
March	24,000	372,500
April	26,500	410,000
May	25,500	395,000

The following information relates to questions 2.4 to 2.8

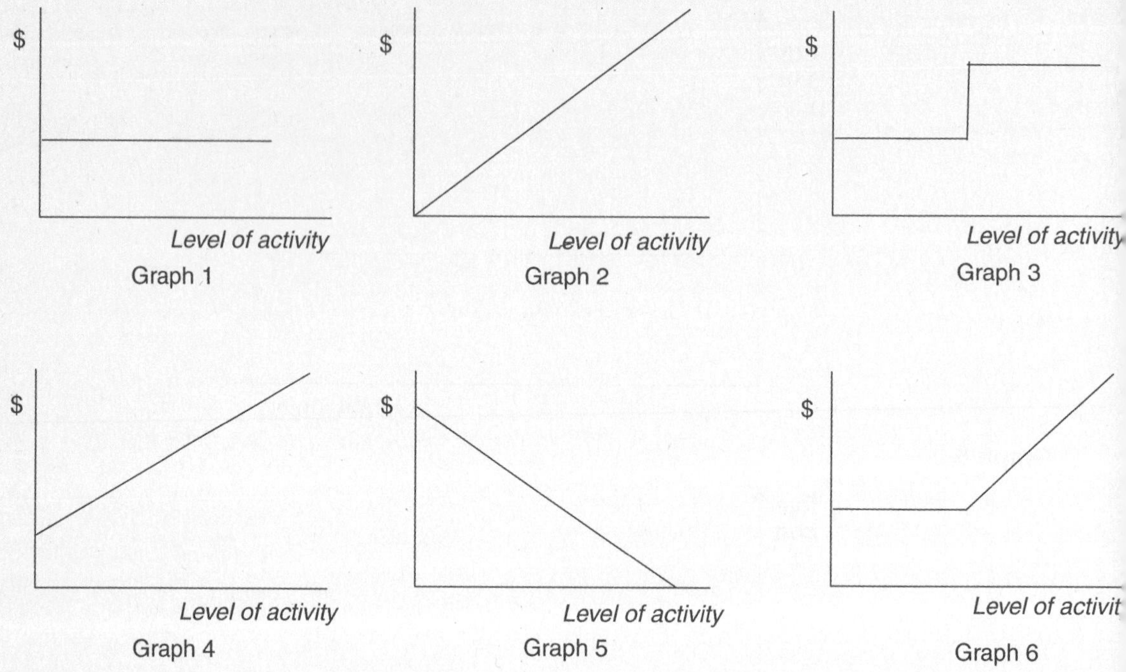

$

Level of activity
Graph 1

$

Level of activity
Graph 2

$

Level of activity
Graph 3

$

Level of activity
Graph 4

$

Level of activity
Graph 5

$

Level of activity
Graph 6

Which one of the above graphs illustrates the costs described in tasks 2.4 to 2.8?

Task 2.4

A variable cost – when the vertical axis represents cost incurred.

☐ Graph 1
☐ Graph 2
☐ Graph 4
☐ Graph 5

Task 2.5

A fixed cost – when the vertical axis represents cost incurred.

☐ Graph 1
☐ Graph 2
☐ Graph 3
☐ Graph 6

Task 2.6

A variable cost – when the vertical axis represents cost per unit.

☐ Graph 1

☐ Graph 2

☐ Graph 3

☐ Graph 6

Task 2.7

A semi-variable cost – when the vertical axis represents cost incurred.

☐ Graph 1

☐ Graph 2

☐ Graph 4

☐ Graph 5

Task 2.8

A step fixed cost – when the vertical axis represents cost incurred.

☐ Graph 3

☐ Graph 4

☐ Graph 5

☐ Graph 6

Task 2.9

A company has recorded the following data in the two most recent periods.

Total costs of production £	Volume of production Units
13,500	700
18,300	1,100

What is the best estimate of the company's fixed costs per period?

☐ £13,500

☐ £13,200

☐ £5,100

☐ £4,800

Task 2.10

We usually classify short-term costs into fixed, variable, step-fixed or semi-variable but in the long run, all costs are:

☐ Fixed

☐ Variable

☐ Step-fixed

☐ Semi-variable

Chapter 3

Task 3.1

Paris Ltd manufactures a product the Lipsy, which requires plastic handles PH5:

- Annual demand 90,000 kilograms.
- Annual holding cost per kilogram £1
- Fixed ordering cost £2

(a) **Calculate the Economic Order Quantity (EOQ) for PH5**

The inventory record shown below for plastic grade PH5 for the month of September has only been fully completed for the first three weeks of the month.

(b) **Complete the entries in the inventory record for the two receipts on 24 and 28 September that were ordered using the EOQ method.**

(c) **Complete ALL entries in the inventory record for the two issues in the month and for the closing balance at the end of September using the FIFO method of issuing inventory. (Show the costs per kilogram (kg) in £s to 3 decimal places; and the total costs in whole £s.)**

Inventory record for plastic grade PH5:

| Date | Receipts | | | Issues | | | Balance | |
	Quantity kgs	Cost per kg (£)	Total cost (£)	Quantity kgs	Cost per kg (£)	Total cost (£)	Quantity Kgs	Total cost (£)
Balance as at 22 September							150	180
24 September		1.398						
26 September				400				
28 September		1.402						
30 September				500				

Task 3.2

Calculate the closing inventory value at 31 March using FIFO by completing the entries in the inventory record below. Enter the cost per unit to 1 decimal place and the total cost to the nearest whole pound.

Inventory record

Date	Receipts			Issues			Balance	
	Quantity kgs	Cost per kg (£)	Total cost (£)	Quantity kgs	Cost per kg (£)	Total cost (£)	Quantity Kgs	Total cost (£)
Balance as at 1 January							4,000	10,000
31 January	1,000		2,000					
15 February				3,000		7,500		
28 February	1,500		3,750					
14 March				500		1,250		

Task 3.3

Using the AVCO method calculate the cost of materials issues and the value of closing inventory using the information below.

Enter your answer onto the inventory record below. Important! Enter the cost per kg to 2 decimal places. Enter the total cost to the nearest whole pound.

January 1	Balance	300 kg	£25 per unit
January 2	Issue	250 kg	
January 12	Receipt	400 kg	£25.75 per unit
January 21	Issue	200 kg	
January 29	Issue	75 kg	

Inventory Record Card								
	Purchases			Requisitions			Balance	
Date	Quantity	Cost	Total cost	Quantity	Cost	Total cost	Quantity	Total cost
	(kg)	£	£		£	£		£
1 Jan								
2 Jan								
12 Jan								
21 Jan								
29 Jan								

. . . .

Task 3.4

A company wishes to minimise its inventory costs. Order costs are £10 per order and holding costs are £0.10 per unit per month. Fall Co estimates **annual** demand to be 5,400 units.

The economic order quantity is ☐ **units** .

. . . .

Task 3.5

The following data relates to component L512:

Ordering costs   £100 per order
Inventory holding costs   £8 per unit per annum
Annual demand   1,225 units

The economic order quantity is ⬚ **units (to the nearest whole unit).**

Task 3.6

The following data relate to inventory item A452:

Average usage   100 units per day

Minimum usage   60 units per day

Maximum usage   130 units per day

Lead time   20-26 days

EOQ   4,000 units

The maximum inventory level was ⬚ **units**

Chapter 4

Task 4.1

Below is a weekly timesheet for one of Paris Ltd's employees, who is paid as follows:

- For a basic seven-hour shift every day from Monday to Friday - basic pay.

- For any overtime in excess of the basic seven hours, on any day from Monday to Friday - the extra hours are paid at time-and-a-third (basic pay plus an overtime premium equal to a third of basic pay).

- For three contracted hours each Saturday morning - basic pay.

- For any hours in excess of three hours on Saturday - the extra hours are paid at double time (basic pay plus an overtime premium equal to basic pay).

- For any hours worked on Sunday - paid at double time (basic pay plus an overtime premium equal to basic pay).

Complete the columns headed Basic pay, Overtime premium and Total pay:

(Notes: Zero figures should be entered in cells where appropriate; Overtime pay is the premium amount paid for the extra hours worked).

Employee's weekly timesheet for week ending 14 May

Employee: H. Hector				Cost Centre: Lipsy calibration			
Employee number: LP100				Basic pay per hour: £9.00			

	Hours spent on production	Hours worked on indirect work	Notes	Basic pay £	Overtime premium £	Total pay £
Monday	6	1	10am-11am setting up of machinery			
Tuesday	3	4	9am-1pm department meeting			
Wednesday	8					
Thursday	8					
Friday	6	1	3pm-4pm health and safety training			
Saturday	4					
Sunday	4					
Total	39	6				

Task 4.2

Paris Ltd is reviewing its overtime payments for employees and has decided to increase basic pay from £9/hr to £10/hr and reduce its payment of overtime as follows. All other terms remain the same.

- For any overtime in excess of the basic seven hours, on any day from Monday to Friday - the extra hours are paid at time-and-a-quarter (basic pay plus an overtime premium equal to a quarter of basic pay).

- For four contracted hours each Saturday morning - basic pay.

- For any hours worked on Sunday - paid at time and a half (basic pay plus an overtime premium equal to half of basic pay).

Recalculate the timesheet for H. Hector for the week ending 14 May, taking these changes into account.

	Hours spent on production	Hours worked on indirect work	Notes	Basic pay £	Overtime premium £	Total pay £
Employee: H. Hector			**Cost Centre:** Lipsy calibration			
Employee number: LP100			**Basic pay per hour:** £10.00			
Monday	6	1	10am-11am setting up of machinery			
Tuesday	3	4	9am-1pm department meeting			
Wednesday	8					
Thursday	8					
Friday	6	1	3pm-4pm health and safety training			
Saturday	4					
Sunday	4					
Total	39	6				

Task 4.3

Paris Ltd has drawn up its payroll records for the month of May. The records show the following details of pay:

	£
Net pay	250,000
PAYE and NIC deductions	62,500
Contributions to company welfare scheme	37,500
Gross pay	350,000

The payroll analysis shows that £275,000 relates to direct labour, and £75,000 is for indirect labour. **The Financial controller has asked you to record the entries in the ledger in the Wages control account.** Remember Paris Ltd is a manufacturing company, so you need to think about work in progress too.

Task 4.4

The ledger clerk has forgotten to complete the other entries needed for wages in the work in progress control account and the production overhead control account. **Input the correct entries in the two control accounts below.** Remember that £275,000 relates to direct labour and £75,000 to indirect labour.

Work in progress control account			
	£		£
31 May	Wages control		

Production overhead control			
	£		£
31 May	Wages control		

Task 4.5

Which one of the following groups of workers would be classified as indirect labour?

☐ Machinists in an organisation manufacturing clothes

☐ Bricklayers in a house building company

☐ Maintenance workers in a shoe factory

Task 4.6

In a typical cost ledger, the double entry for indirect labour cost incurred is:

	DEBIT	Wages control	CREDIT	Overhead control
☐	DEBIT	Admin overhead control	CREDIT	Wages control
☐	DEBIT	Overhead control	CREDIT	Wages control
☐	DEBIT	Wages control	CREDIT	Admin overhead control

Chapter 5

Task 5.1

Paris Ltd has set its budgets and estimated its budgeted overheads and activity levels as follows:

	Silicon moulding	Silicon extrusion
Budgeted overheads (£)	450,000	352,520
Budgeted direct labour hours	25,350	20,475
Budgeted machine hours	8,750	6,350

(a) **What would be the budgeted overhead absorption rate for each department, if this were set based on their both being heavily automated?**

☐ Silicon moulding £18/hour, Silicon extrusion £17/hour

☐ Silicon moulding £51/hour, Silicon extrusion £17/hour

☐ Silicon moulding £51/hour, Silicon extrusion £56/hour

☐ Silicon moulding £18/hour, Silicon extrusion £56/hour

(b) **What would be the budgeted overhead absorption rate for each department, if this were set based on their both being labour intensive?**

☐ Silicon moulding £51/hour, Silicon extrusion £17/hour

☐ Silicon moulding £18/hour, Silicon extrusion £17/hour

☐ Silicon moulding £18/hour, Silicon extrusion £56/hour

☐ Silicon moulding £51/hour, Silicon extrusion £56/hour

Additional data

At the end of the quarter actual overheads incurred were found to be:

	Silicon moulding	Silicon extrusion
Actual overheads (£)	425,799	354,416

(c) **Assuming that exactly the same amount of overheads was absorbed as budgeted, what were the under- or over-absorptions in the quarter?**

☐ Silicon moulding over-absorbed £24,201, Silicon extrusion over-absorbed £1,896

☐ Silicon moulding over-absorbed £24,201, Silicon extrusion under-absorbed £1,896

☐ Silicon moulding under-absorbed £24,201, Silicon extrusion under-absorbed £1,896

☐ Silicon moulding under-absorbed £24,201, Silicon extrusion over-absorbed £1,896

Task 5.2

The financial controller at Paris Ltd has looked at the overhead absorption rates in the two cost centres, and wants a single rate for labour hours and for machinery across the two centres. She has chosen £20/hr for labour hours and £55/hr for machinery. **Recalculate the budgeted direct labour hours and machine hours based on these rates.** Refer to the table below from the last task:

	Silicon moulding	Silicon extrusion
Budgeted overheads (£)	450,000	352,520
Budgeted direct labour hours		
Budgeted machine hours		

Task 5.3

(a) At the end of the quarter you have been asked to recalculate the overhead absorbed using the new rates and the following actual hours for labour and machinery:

	Silicon moulding	Silicon extrusion
Actual direct labour hours	21,222	17,144
Actual machine hours	8,459	6,501
Budgeted overhead absorbed – labour hrs		
Budgeted overhead absorbed – machine hrs		

(b) Using the actual overheads in Task 5.1, calculate any differences between the actual overheads at the end of the quarter and the overheads absorbed in part(a).

	Silicon moulding	Silicon extrusion
Actual overheads (£)		
Difference - labour hours		
Difference - machine hours		

Task 5.4

Over-absorbed overheads occur when

☐ Absorbed overheads exceed actual overheads

☐ Absorbed overheads exceed budgeted overheads

☐ Actual overheads exceed budgeted overheads

The following information relates to task 5.5 and 5.6

A company has the following actual and budgeted data for year 4.

	Budget	Actual
Labour hours	8,000 hrs	9,000 hrs
Variable production overhead per unit	£3	£3
Fixed production overheads	£360,000	£432,000
Sales	6,000 units	8,000 units

Overheads are absorbed using a rate per unit, based on budgeted labour hours.

Task 5.5

The fixed production overhead absorbed during year 4 was:

☐ £384,000

☐ £405,000

☐ £432,000

☐ £459,000

Task 5.6

Fixed production overhead was:

☐ under absorbed by £27,000

☐ under absorbed by £72,000

☐ under absorbed by £75,000

☐ over absorbed by £27,000

Chapter 6

Task 6.1

Paris Ltd's budgeted overheads for the next financial year are:

	£	£
Depreciation of plant and equipment		2,010,375
Power for production machinery		1,787,500
Rent and rates		261,250
Light and heat		57,750
Indirect labour costs:		
Maintenance	253,750	
Stores	90,125	
General Administration	600,250	
Total indirect labour cost		944,125

The following information is also available:

Department	Net book value of plant and equipment	Production machinery power usage (KwH)	Floor space (square metres)	Number of employees
Production centres:				
Silicon moulding	3,600,000	1,145,000		15
Silicon extrusion	4,400,000	2,430,000		16
Support cost centres:				
Maintenance			8,000	4
Stores			10,000	5
General Administration			10,000	6
Total	8,000,000	3,575,000	28,000	46

Overheads are allocated or apportioned on the most appropriate basis. The total overheads of the support cost centres are then reapportioned to the two production centres using the direct method.

- 35% of the Maintenance cost centre's time is spent maintaining production machinery in the Silicon moulding production centre, and the remainder in the Silicon extrusion production centre.

- The Stores cost centre makes 40% of its issues to the Silicon moulding production centre, and 60% to the Silicon extrusion production centre.

- General Administration supports the two production centres equally.

- There is no reciprocal servicing between the three support cost centres.

Complete the table showing the apportionment and reapportionment of overheads to the two production centres. Round to the nearest pound.

	Basis of apportionment	Silicon moulding £	Silicon extrusion £	Mainten ance £	Stores £	General Admin £	Totals £
Depreciation of plant and equipment	NBV of Plant and equipment						
Power for production machinery	Production machinery power usage (KwH)						
Rent and rates	Floor space						
Light and heat	Floor space						
Indirect labour	Allocated						
Totals							
Reapportion Maintenance							
Reapportion Stores							
Reapportion General Admin							
Total overheads to production centres							

Task 6.2

(a) The financial controller at Paris Ltd is reviewing the basis of allocating the costs of the two production centres, and is considering using the number of employees instead of NBV and power usage. Recalculate the allocations and apportionments using headcount as a basis for these two cost centres. She has also decided that the silicon moulding cost centre uses far more general admin than the extrusion cost centre, and wants you to recalculate the apportionments using a ratio of 65:35. Use the dropdown screen to remind you of the data in the task.

Dropdown screen

Paris Ltd's budgeted overheads for the next financial year are:

	£	£
Depreciation of plant and equipment		2,010,375
Power for production machinery		1,787,500
Rent and rates		261,250
Light and heat		57,750
Indirect labour costs:		
Maintenance	253,750	
Stores	90,125	
General Administration	600,250	
Total indirect labour cost		944,125

The following information is also available:

Department	Net book value of plant and equipment	Production machinery power usage (KwH)	Floor space (square metres)	Number of employees
Production centres:				
Silicon moulding	3,600,000	1,145,000		15
Silicon extrusion	4,400,000	2,430,000		16
Support cost centres:				
Maintenance			8,000	4

Department	Net book value of plant and equipment	Production machinery power usage (KwH)	Floor space (square metres)	Number of employees
Stores			10,000	5
General Administration			10,000	6
Total	8,000,000	3,575,000	28,000	46

Overheads are allocated or apportioned on the most appropriate basis. The total overheads of the support cost centres are then reapportioned to the two production centres using the direct method.

- 35% of the Maintenance cost centre's time is spent maintaining production machinery in the Silicon moulding production centre, and the remainder in the Silicon extrusion production centre.

- The Stores cost centre makes 40% of its issues to the Silicon moulding production centre, and 60% to the Silicon extrusion production centre.

- General Administration supports the two production centres, with 65% of its costs attributable to Silicon moulding and 35% attributable to Silicon extrusion.

- There is no reciprocal servicing between the three support cost centres.

Complete the table showing the apportionment and reapportionment of overheads to the two production centres.

	Basis of apportionment	Silicon moulding £	Silicon extrusion £	Mainten ance £	Stores £	General Admin £	Totals £
Depreciation of plant and equipment	Headcount						
Power for production machinery	Headcount						
Rent and rates	Floor space						
Light and heat	Floor space						
Indirect labour	Allocated						

	Basis of apportionment	Silicon moulding £	Silicon extrusion £	Mainten ance £	Stores £	General Admin £	Totals £
Totals							
Reapportion Maintenance							
Reapportion Stores							
Reapportion General Admin							
Total overheads to production centres							

(b) **If you were the manager in charge of the silicon moulding cost centre would you be happy with the revised allocations?**

Chapter 7

Task 7.1

Drag and drop the correct entries into the box below to match the correct cost unit to a service:

1. Occupied bed-night
2. Patient-day
3. Meal served
4. Passenger/kilometre, tonne/kilometre
5. Full-time student

Service	Cost unit
Road, rail and air transport services	
Hotels	
Education	
Hospitals	
Catering establishments	

Task 7.2

Petra Jones is a builder who has issued a quote for a conservatory. Now the job is completed, she would like you to calculate any variances that have arisen. **State whether each variance is favourable or adverse (unfavourable).** The details are in the table below. Input your answers into the right hand column.

Job number 03456

	Budget £	Actual £	Variance F/A £
Direct materials			
Plasterboard	3,600.00	3,500.00	
Wood & door frames	4,750.00	4,802.00	
Insulation	1,050.00	1,145.00	
Electrical fittings	320.00	300.00	
Windows	2,220.00	2,576.00	
Paint	270.00	250.00	
Direct labour			
Construction	554.00	641.00	
Electrical	224.00	160.00	

	Budget £	Actual £	Variance F/A £
Decorating	165.00	205.00	
Direct expenses			
Hire of specialist lathe	240.00	240.00	
Overheads (based upon direct labour hours)			
84/90 hours @ £15.00	<u>1,260.00</u>	<u>1,350.00</u>	

Task 7.3

(a) Petra Jones has also asked you to highlight any variances above 5% for further investigation. Use the table below to make your calculations. Enter the percentages to one decimal place.

(b) She also wants you to calculate the profit on the job, comparing this with the original quotation made based on 20% of total cost.

(c) Calculate the percentage variance between the original profit and the final profit figure. Give your answer to 1 decimal place.

	Budget £	Actual £	Variance F/A £	%
Direct materials				
Plasterboard	3,600.00	3,500.00	100F	
Wood & door frames	4,750.00	4,802.00	52A	
Insulation	1,050.00	1,145.00	95A	
Electrical fittings	320.00	300.00	20F	
Windows	2,220.00	2,576.00	356A	
Paint	270.00	250.00	20F	
Direct labour				
Construction	554.00	641.00	87A	
Electrical	224.00	160.00	64F	
Decorating	165.00	205.00	40A	
Direct expenses				
Hire of specialist lathe	240.00	240.00	0	
Overheads (based upon direct labour hours)				
84/90 hours @ £15.00	1,260.00	1,350.00	90A	
Total cost	14,653.00			
Profit	2,930.60			
Net price	17,583.60			
VAT at 20%	3,516.72			
Total price	21,100.32			

Task 7.4

Which of the following are characteristics of service costing?

☐ High levels of indirect costs as a proportion of total cost

☐ Cost units are often intangible

☐ Use of composite cost units

☐ Use of equivalent units

Chapter 8

Task 8.1

The teeming and lading department of Paris Ltd uses process costing for some of its products.

The process account for October for one particular process has been partly completed but the following information is also relevant:

Two employees worked on this process during October. Each employee worked 37 hours per week for 4 weeks and was paid £12.50 per hour.

Overheads are absorbed on the basis of £10.50 per labour hour.

Paris Ltd expects a normal loss of 5% during this process, which it then sells for scrap at 70p per kg.

(a) Complete the process account below for December.

Description	Kgs	Unit cost £	Total cost £	Description	Kgs	Unit cost £	Total cost £
Material TL4	700	1.35		Normal loss		0.70	
Material TL3	350	1.50		Output			
Material TL9	400	1.25					
Labour							
Overheads							

(b) Identify the correct journal entries for an abnormal loss.

	Debit	Credit
Abnormal loss account		
Process account		

Task 8.2

Paris Ltd has reviewed its labour costs and decided to hire two cheaper employees, paying them £9.50 per hour. However they are less experienced and take longer, so they each work 40 hours per week for four weeks. The normal loss goes up to 10% during the process. Overheads continue to be absorbed at £10.50 per labour hour.

Recalculate the process account to take account of these changes.

Description	Kgs	Unit cost £	Total cost £	Description	Kgs	Unit cost £	Total cost £
Material TL4	700	1.35		Normal loss		0.70	
Material TL3	350	1.50		Output			
Material TL9	400	1.25					
Labour							
Overheads							

Do you think the decision made by management is a good one?

Task 8.3

Paris Ltd makes a product which goes through several processes. The following information is available for the month of June:

	Kg
Opening WIP	4,500
Input	54,300
Normal loss	400
Transferred to finished goods	60,400

What was the abnormal gain in June?

- [ ] 2,600 kg
- [ ] 3,000 kg
- [ ] 2,000 kg
- [ ] 2,560 kg

Task 8.4

A food manufacturing process has a normal wastage of 10% of input. In a period, 3,000 kg of material were input and there was an abnormal loss of 75 kg. No inventories are held at the beginning or end of the process.

The quantity of good production achieved was [   ] **kg**

....

Task 8.5

A company makes a product, which passes through a single process.

Details of the process for the last period are as follows:

Materials   5,000 kg at 50p per kg

Normal losses are 10% of input in the process, and without further processing any losses can be sold as scrap for 20p per kg.

The output for the period was 4,200 kg from the process.

There was no work in progress at the beginning or end of the period.

(a) The value credited to the process account for the scrap value of the normal loss for the period will be £ [   ] **(to the nearest £)**

(b) The abnormal loss for the period is [   ] **kg**

....

Chapter 9

Task 9.1

Paris Ltd has prepared a forecast for the next quarter for one of its small components, PA01. This component is produced in batches, and the forecast is based on producing and selling 3,000 batches.

One of the customers of Paris Ltd has indicated that it may be significantly increasing its order level for component PA01 for the next quarter, and it appears that activity levels of 3,750 batches and 5,000 batches are feasible.

The semi-variable costs should be calculated using the high-low method. If 7,500 batches are sold the total semi-variable cost will be £18,450, and there is a constant unit variable cost up to this volume.

Complete the table below and calculate the estimated profit per batch of PA01 at the different activity levels.

Batches produced and sold	3,000	3,750	5,000
	£	£	£
Sales revenue	60,000		
Variable costs:			
• Direct materials	5,700		
• Direct labour	27,000		
• Overheads	9,300		
Semi-variable costs:	9,450		
• Variable element			
• Fixed element			
Total cost	51,450		
Total profit	8,550		
Profit per batch (to 2 decimal places)	2.85		

Task 9.2

(a) The financial controller at Paris Ltd has just informed you of the following cost increases and asked you to recalculate the budget at the three activity levels.

Direct materials £2.00/kg. 1 kg is used in each PA01.

Direct labour £10/hr. It takes 1 hour to make a PA01.

Overheads are now £3.20 per PA01.

Complete the table below and calculate the estimated profit per batch of PA01 at the different activity levels.

Batches produced and sold	3,000	3,750	5,000
	£	£	£
Sales revenue	60,000		
Variable costs:			
• Direct materials			
• Direct labour			
• Overheads			
Semi-variable costs:	9,450		
• Variable element			
• Fixed element			
Total cost			
Total profit			
Profit per batch (to 2 decimal places)			

(b) She has also asked you to recalculate the profit per batch, as Paris Ltd is considering whether to stop production of all batches where the profit per batch is less than £2.

Task 9.3

A customer has put in an order for 4,000 batches. Production is stopped where the profit per batch is less than £2. Recommend to management whether Paris Ltd should go ahead with the order. **Fill in the table below:**

Batches produced and sold	3,000	4,000
	£	£
Sales revenue	60,000	
Variable costs:		
• Direct materials	6,000	
• Direct labour	30,000	
• Overheads	9,600	
Semi-variable costs:		
• Variable element	6,000	
• Fixed element	3,450	
Total cost	55,050	
Total profit	4,950	
Profit per batch (to 2 decimal places)	1.65	

Choose the correct option below.

Paris Ltd should accept/reject the order for 4,000 units

Chapter 10

Task 10.1

Paris Ltd has the following original budget and actual performance for product SHEP for the year ending 30 September:

	Budget	Actual
Volume sold	150,000	156,000
	£'000	£'000
Sales revenue	1,200	1,326
Less costs:		
Direct materials	375	372
Direct labour	450	444
Overheads	225	250
Operating profit	150	260

Both direct materials and direct labour are variable costs, but the overheads are fixed.

Complete the table below to show a flexed budget and the resulting variances against this budget for the year. Show the actual variance amount for sales, each cost, and operating profit, in the column headed 'Variance' and indicate whether this is Favourable or Adverse by entering F or A in the final column. If neither F nor A enter 0.

	Flexed Budget	Actual	Variance	Favourable F or Adverse A
Volume sold		156,000		
	£'000	£'000	£'000	
Sales revenue		1,326		
Less costs:				
Direct materials		372		
Direct labour		444		
Overheads		250		
Operating profit		260		

Task 10.2

The Managing director of Paris Ltd has asked you to explain why the actual outcome was better than budgeted. He wants you to do some calculations and suggest reasons why the revenues and costs may be better than budgeted. Input your calculations to two decimal places into the table below, in the two right hand columns. Ignore overheads.

	Flexed Budget	Actual	Budget unit cost/revenue	Actual unit cost/revenue
Volume sold	156,000	156,000		
	£'000	£'000		
Sales revenue	1,248	1,326		
Less costs:				
Direct materials	390	372		
Direct labour	468	444		
Overheads	225	250		
Operating profit	165	260		

Are the following true or false?

The unit selling price difference may be due to a rise in the sales price not planned in the budget.

True/False

The unit selling price difference may be due to fewer bulk discounts to customers.

True/False

The materials unit price difference may be due to bulk buying discounts.

True/False

The materials unit price difference may be due to a cheaper source of supply

True/False

The labour cost difference may be due to having more lower paid employees.

True/False

The labour cost difference may be due to efficiency savings.

True/False

Chapter 11

Task 11.1

Drag and drop the correct entries into the journal below to record the following transactions:

1. production overheads absorbed into production
2. indirect labour transferred to production overheads
3. completed WIP transferred to finished goods
4. direct materials issued to production

The choices are:

Debit: WIP, Credit: Production overheads

Debit: Production overheads, Credit: Wages

Debit: Finished goods, Credit: WIP

Debit: WIP, Credit: Materials

Debit: WIP, Credit: Finished goods

Debit: Production overheads, Credit: WIP

Production overheads absorbed into production		
Indirect labour transferred to production overheads		
Completed WIP transferred to finished goods		
Direct materials issued to production		

Task 11.2

Drag and drop the correct entries into the journal below to record the following transactions for overheads:

Transaction 1.   Over-absorbed: absorbed greater than incurred
Transaction 2.   Under-absorbed: incurred greater than absorbed

The drag and drop choices are:

- Debit: production overheads, Credit: income statement
- Debit: income statement, Credit: production overheads

	Drag and drop choice
Transaction 1	
Transaction 2	

Task 11.3

A company operates an integrated accounting system.

The accounting entries for the issue to production of indirect materials from inventory would be:

DEBIT	CREDIT
☐ Work in progress account	Materials control account
☐ Materials control account	Production overhead control account
☐ Production overhead control account	Materials control account
☐ Cost of sales account	Materials control account

Chapter 12

Task 12.1

Paris Ltd uses absorption costing, but is looking at adopting marginal costing across some of its products. The details for the PA121 are below:

Direct materials	£8.50
Direct labour	£17.00
Variable overheads	£3.00
Fixed overheads	£850,000

Overheads are absorbed on the machine hour basis, and it is estimated that in the next accounting period machine hours will total 250,000. Each unit requires two hours of machine time.

What is the cost per unit using:

(a) absorption costing
(b) marginal costing?

Task 12.2

Drag and drop the correct answer into the sentence below:

1. more for absorption costing
2. the same for both types of costing
3. less for absorption costing

In the long run, total profit for a company will be [   ] whether marginal costing or absorption costing is used.

Task 12.3

Drag and drop the correct answer into the sentence below:

1. absorption costing, marginal costing
2. marginal costing, absorption costing

It might be argued that [   ] is preferable **to** [   ] **in management accounting**, in order to be consistent with the requirement of current accounting standards and financial reporting.

BPP
LEARNING MEDIA

Task 12.4

Cost and selling price details for product Z are as follows.

	£
Direct materials	6.00
Direct labour	7.50
Variable overhead	2.50
Fixed overhead absorption rate	5.00
	21.00
Profit	9.00
Selling price	30.00

Budgeted production for the month was 5,000 units although the company managed to produce 5,800 units, selling 5,200 of them and incurring fixed overhead costs of £27,400.

(a) **What was the marginal costing profit for the month?**

☐ £45,400 ☐ £53,800

☐ £46,800 ☐ £72,800

(b) **What was the absorption costing profit for the month?**

☐ £45,200 ☐ £46,800

☐ £45,400 ☐ £48,400

Chapter 13

Task 13.1

The COLIN has a selling price of £22 per unit with a total variable cost of £17 per unit. Paris Ltd estimates that the fixed costs per quarter associated with this product are £45,000.

(a) Calculate the budgeted breakeven, in units, for product COLIN.

units

(b) Calculate the budgeted breakeven, in £s, for product COLIN.

£

(c) Complete the table below to show the budgeted margin of safety in units and the margin of safety percentage (to the nearest whole %) and the margin of safety in revenue if Paris Ltd sells 9,500 units or 10,500 units of product COLIN.

Units of COLIN sold	9,500	10,500
Margin of safety (units)		
Margin of safety percentage		
Margin of safety revenue		

(d) If Paris Ltd wishes to make a profit of £20,000, how many units of COLIN must it sell?

units

(e) If Paris Ltd increases the selling price of COLIN by £1 what will be the impact on the breakeven point and the margin of safety, assuming no change in the number of units sold?

☐ The breakeven point will decrease and the margin of safety will increase.

☐ The margin of safety will stay the same but the breakeven point will increase.

☐ The breakeven point will decrease and the margin of safety will stay the same.

☐ The margin of safety will decrease and the breakeven point will decrease.

Task 13.2

(a) Paris Ltd has decided to limit the production of the COLIN to 8,000 units per quarter. If the selling price and variable costs remain the same, what is the maximum fixed costs per quarter to breakeven? Remember the selling price is £22 per unit and the variable cost is £17 per unit.

(b) Calculate the revised budgeted breakeven, in £s, for product COLIN if fixed costs are £30,000 per quarter.

£

(c) Complete the table below to show the budgeted margin of safety in units and the margin of safety percentage (to the nearest whole %) if Paris Ltd sells 6,500 units or 7,000 units of product COLIN. Base this on your answer in part (b).

Units of COLIN sold	6,500	7,000
	£	£
Margin of safety (units)		
Margin of safety percentage		

(d) If Paris Ltd wishes to make a profit of £10,000, how many units of COLIN must it sell? Is it possible to make this level of profit? Base this on the data in parts (b) and (c)

units

....

Task 13.3

A company makes a single product and incurs fixed costs of £30,000 per month. Variable cost per unit is £5 and each unit sells for £15. Monthly sales demand is 7,000 units.

The breakeven point in terms of monthly sales units is:

☐ 2,000 units

☐ 3,000 units

☐ 4,000 units

☐ 6,000 units

....

Task 13.4

A company manufactures a single product for which cost and selling price data are as follows.

Selling price per unit   £12

Variable cost per unit   £8

Fixed costs per month   £96,000

Budgeted monthly sales   30,000 units

The margin of safety, expressed as a percentage of budgeted monthly sales, is (to the nearest whole number):

☐ 20%

☐ 25%

☐ 73%

☐ 125%

Task 13.5

Information concerning K Co's single product is as follows.

	£ per unit
Selling price	6.00
Variable production cost	1.20
Variable selling cost	0.40
Fixed production cost	4.00
Fixed selling cost	0.80

Budgeted production and sales for the year are 10,000 units.

(a) What is the company's breakeven point, to the nearest whole unit?

☐ 8,000 units

☐ 8,333 units

☐ 10,000 units

☐ 10,909 units

(b) **How many units must be sold if K Co wants to achieve a profit of £11,000 for the year?**

☐ 2,500 units

☐ 9,833 units

☐ 10,625 units

☐ 13,409 units

Chapter 14

Task 14.1

Beanie Ltd has a stamping machine nearing the end of its useful life and is considering purchasing a replacement machine.

Estimates have been made for the initial capital cost, sales income and operating costs of the replacement machine, which is expected to have a useful life of four years:

	Year 0 £'000	Year 1 £'000	Year 2 £'000	Year 3 £'000	Year 4 £'000
Capital expenditure	1,000				
Other cash flows:					
Sales income		350	400	400	350
Operating costs		100	110	120	130

The company appraises capital investment projects using a 11% cost of capital.

(a) **Complete the table below and calculate the net present value of the proposed replacement machine (to the nearest £'000):**

	Year 0 £'000	Year 1 £'000	Year 2 £'000	Year 3 £'000	Year 4 £'000
Capital expenditure					
Sales income					
Operating costs					
Net cash flows					
PV factors	1.0000	0.9009	0.8116	0.7312	0.6587
Discounted cash flows (to nearest £)					
Net present value					

The net present value is ⬛▾

Picklist

Positive
Negative

(b) Calculate the payback period of the proposed replacement machine to the nearest whole month.

The payback period is [   ] year(s) and [   ] month(s).

....

Task 14.2

The Managing Director of Beanie Ltd has been looking at your calculations for the replacement machine. **He wants to know the maximum he should pay for a replacement machine to make sure the NPV at least breaks even.**

....

Task 14.3

It has now been decided to purchase the replacement stamping machine, but the managing director wants you to use a lower rate for the cost of capital and he has settled on 7%. He also wants you to use a figure of £810,000 for the cost of the replacement machine. All other cash flows are as before.

	Year 0 £'000	Year 1 £'000	Year 2 £'000	Year 3 £'000	Year 4 £'000
Capital expenditure	810				
Other cash flows:					
Sales income		350	400	400	350
Operating costs		100	110	120	130

The company appraises capital investment projects using a 7% cost of capital.

47

Complete the table below and calculate the net present value of the proposed replacement machine (to the nearest £'000):

	Year 0 £'000	Year 1 £'000	Year 2 £'000	Year 3 £'000	Year 4 £'000
Capital expenditure					
Sales income					
Operating costs					
Net cash flows					
PV factors	1.0000	0.9346	0.8734	0.8163	0.7629
Discounted cash flows					
Net present value					

The net present value is [▼]

Picklist

Positive
Negative

Answer bank

Answer bank

Costs and Revenues Answer bank

Chapter 1

Task 1.1

	Financial accounting	Management accounting
Users	External to the organisation	Internal management
Timing	Annual	When required
Type of information	Historic	Historic and future
Format	Specified by law	To be useful

Task 1.2

```
COST CARD
                                    £

Direct Materials                    X
Direct labour                       X
Direct expenses                     X
Prime cost                          X
Production overheads                X
Production cost                     X
Non-production overheads
    -  selling and distribution     X
    -  administration               X
    -  finance                      X
Total cost                          X
```

Task 1.3

The correct answer is: A maintenance assistant in a factory maintenance department.

The maintenance assistant is not working directly on the organisation's output but is performing an indirect task. All the other three options describe tasks that involve working directly on the output.

Task 1.4

The correct answer is: Costs and Revenues

Profit centre managers are normally responsible for costs and revenues only.

Task 1.5

The correct answer is: Staples to fix the fabric to the seat of a chair

Indirect costs are those which **cannot be easily identified** with a specific cost unit. Although the staples could probably be identified with a specific chair, the cost is likely to be relatively insignificant. The expense of tracing such costs does not usually justify the possible benefits from calculating more accurate direct costs. The cost of the staples would therefore be treated as an indirect cost, to be included as a part of the overhead absorption rate.

The other options all represent significant costs which can be traced to a specific cost unit. Therefore they are classified as direct costs.

Task 1.6

The correct answer is: The total of direct costs

Prime cost is the total of direct material, direct labour and direct expenses.

All costs incurred in manufacturing a product describes total production cost, including absorbed production overhead. **The material cost of a product** is only a part of prime cost.

Chapter 2

Task 2.1

	Drag and drop choice
Production cost	**Factory heat and light, Depreciation of plant and machinery**
Selling and distribution cost	**Sales Director's salary, Depreciation of delivery vans, Fuel and oil for delivery vans**
Administration cost	**Finance Director's salary**

....

Task 2.2

Graph A – variable cost per unit

Graph B – total fixed cost across level of activity

....

Task 2.3

	Output (units)	Total cost £
Highest	26,500	410,000
Lowest	16,000	252,500
Increase	10,500	157,500

Variable cost per unit = 157,500/10,500 = £15 per unit

Fixed cost

16,000 × £15	= £240,000
£252,500 - £240,000	= £12,500
OR	
26,500 × £15	= £397,500
£410,000 - £397,500	= £12,500

....

Task 2.4

The correct answer is Graph 2. Graph 2 shows that costs increase in line with activity levels.

Task 2.5

The correct answer is Graph 1. Graph 1 shows that fixed costs remain the same whatever the level of activity.

Task 2.6

The correct answer is Graph 1. Graph 1 shows that cost per unit remains the same at different levels of activity.

Task 2.7

The correct answer is Graph 4. Graph 4 shows that semi-variable costs have a fixed element and a variable element.

Task 2.8

The correct answer is Graph 3. Graph 3 shows that the step fixed costs go up in 'steps' as the level of activity increases.

Task 2.9

The correct answer is: £5,100

	Units	£
High output	1,100	18,300
Low output	700	13,500
Variable cost	400	4,800

Variable cost per unit £4,800/£400 = £12 per unit

Fixed costs = £18,300 − (£12 × 1,100) = £5,100

Therefore the correct answer is £5,100.

£13,500 is the total cost for an activity of 700 units

£13,200 is the total variable cost for 1,100 units (1,100 × £12)

£4,800 is the difference between the costs incurred at the two activity levels recorded

Task 2.10

The correct answer is variable. In the long run, all costs are variable.

Chapter 3

Task 3.1

(a) The EOQ is 600 kgs = $\sqrt{\dfrac{[2 \times 90,000 \times 2]}{1}}$

(b) and (c) Inventory record card – FIFO

Date	Receipts			Issues			Balance	
	Quantity kgs	Cost per kg (£)	Total cost (£)	Quantity kgs	Cost per kg (£)	Total cost (£)	Quantity Kgs	Total cost (£)
Balance as at 22 September							150	180
24 September	600	1.398	839				750	1,019
26 September				400	1.2/1.398	530	350	489
28 September	600	1.402	841				950	1,330
30 September				500	1.398/1.402	700	450	630

Task 3.2

Inventory record card

Date	Receipts Quantity kgs	Receipts Cost per kg (£)	Receipts Total cost (£)	Issues Quantity kgs	Issues Cost per kg (£)	Issues Total cost (£)	Balance Quantity Kgs	Balance Total cost (£)
Balance as at 1 January							4,000	10,000
31 January	1,000	2.0	2,000				5,000	12,000
15 February				3,000	2.5	7,500	2,000	4,500
28 February	1,500	2.5	3,750				3,500	8,250
14 March				500	2.5	1,250	3,000	7,000

Task 3.3

Inventory record card – AVCO

Inventory Record Card								
	Purchases			Requisitions			Balance	
Date	Quantity (kg)	Cost £	Total cost £	Quantity	Cost £	Total cost £	Quantity	Total cost £
1 Jan							300	7,500
2 Jan				250	25.00	6,250	50	1,250
12 Jan	400	25.75	10,300				450	11,550
21 Jan				200	25.67	5,134	250	6,416
29 Jan				75	25.67	1,925	175	4,491

Task 3.4

The economic order quantity is $\boxed{300}$ units.

The formula for the economic order quantity (EOQ) is

$$EOQ = \sqrt{\frac{2cd}{h}}$$

With c   = £10

d   = 5,400 ÷ 12 = 450 per month

h   = £0.10

$$EOQ = \sqrt{\frac{2 \times £10 \times 450}{£0.10}}$$

$$= \sqrt{90,000}$$

= 300 units

. . . .

Task 3.5

The economic order quantity is $\boxed{175}$ units (to the nearest whole unit).

$$EOQ = \sqrt{\frac{2cd}{h}}$$

$$= \sqrt{\frac{2 \times £100 \times 1,225}{£8}}$$

$$= \sqrt{30,625}$$

= 175 units

. . . .

Task 3.6

The maximum inventory level was $\boxed{6,180}$ units

Reorder level   = maximum usage × maximum lead time

                            = 130 × 26 = 3,380 units

Maximum level   = reorder level + reorder quantity – (minimum usage × minimum lead
time)

                            = 3,380 + 4,000 – (60 × 20)

                            = 6,180 units.

. . . .

Chapter 4

Task 4.1

Employee's weekly timesheet for week ending 14 May

Employee: H. Hector			Cost Centre: Lipsy calibration			
Employee number: LP100			Basic pay per hour: £9.00			
	Hours spent on production	Hours worked on indirect work	Notes	Basic pay £	Overtime premium £	Total pay £
Monday	6	1	10am-11am setting up of machinery	63	0	63
Tuesday	3	4	9am-1pm department meeting	63	0	63
Wednesday	8			72	3	75
Thursday	8			72	3	75
Friday	6	1	3pm-4pm health and safety training	63	0	63
Saturday	4			36	9	45
Sunday	4			36	36	72
Total	**39**	**6**		405	51	456

Task 4.2

Employee's weekly timesheet for week ending 14 May

Employee: H. Hector			Cost Centre: Lipsy calibration			
Employee number: LP100			Basic pay per hour: £10.00			
	Hours spent on production	Hours worked on indirect work	Notes	Basic pay £	Overtime premium £	Total pay £
Monday	6	1	10am-11am setting up of machinery	70	0	70
Tuesday	3	4	9am-1pm department meeting	70	0	70
Wednesday	8			80	2.50	82.50
Thursday	8			80	2.50	82.50
Friday	6	1	3pm-4pm health and safety training	70	0	70
Saturday	4			40	0	40
Sunday	4			40	20	60
Total	39	6		450	25	475

Task 4.3

These details are recorded in the wages control account as follows:

Wages control account

	£		£
Bank	250,000	WIP	275,000
HM Revenue & Customs	62,500	Production overhead control	75,000
Welfare scheme			
Contributions	37,500		
	350,000		350,000

Task 4.4

Work in progress control account

		£		£
31 May	Wages control	275,000		

Production overhead control

		£		£
31 May	Wages control	75,000		

....

Task 4.5

The correct answer is: Maintenance workers in a shoe factory.

....

Task 4.6

✓	DEBIT	Overhead control	CREDIT	Wages control

Indirect wages are 'collected' in the overhead control account, for subsequent absorption into work in progress.

....

Chapter 5

Task 5.1

(a) The correct answer is: Silicon moulding £51/hour, Silicon extrusion £56/hour
(b) The correct answer is: Silicon moulding £18/hour, Silicon extrusion £17/hour
(c) The correct answer is: Silicon moulding over-absorbed £24,201, Silicon extrusion under-absorbed £1,896

Task 5.2

	Silicon moulding	Silicon extrusion
Budgeted overheads (£)	450,000	352,520
Budgeted direct labour hours	22,500	17,626
Budgeted machine hours	8,182	6,409

Task 5.3

(a)

	Silicon moulding	Silicon extrusion
Actual direct labour hours	21,222	17,144
Actual machine hours	8,459	6,501
Budgeted overhead absorbed – labour hrs	424,440	342,880
Budgeted overhead absorbed – machine hrs	465,245	357,555

(b)

	Silicon moulding	Silicon extrusion
Actual overheads (£)	425,799	354,416
Difference – labour hrs	1,359	11,536
Difference – machine hrs	39,446	3,139

Task 5.4

The correct answer is: Absorbed overheads exceed actual overheads.

Absorbed overheads exceeding budgeted overheads could lead to under-absorbed overheads if actual overheads far exceeded both budgeted overheads and the overhead absorbed. Actual overheads exceeding budgeted overheads could lead to under-absorbed overheads if overhead absorbed does not increase in line with actual overhead incurred.

Task 5.5

The correct answer is: £405,000

Budgeted absorption rate for fixed overhead	= £360,000/8,000
	= £45 per hour
Fixed overhead absorbed	= 9,000 hours × £45
	= £405,000

If you selected £384,000 you based your absorption calculations on sales units instead of labour hours.

If you selected £432,000 you calculated the correct figure for fixed overhead absorbed but also added the variable overheads.

£459,000 is the figure for actual total overhead incurred.

Task 5.6

The correct answer is: under-absorbed by £27,000

Actual fixed overhead incurred	= £432,000
Fixed overhead absorbed	= £405,000 (from task 5.5)
Fixed overhead under absorbed	= £27,000

If you selected under-absorbed by £72,000, you simply calculated the difference between the budgeted and actual fixed overhead. If you selected under-absorbed by £75,000, you based your absorption calculations on sales units instead of production units. If you selected over-absorbed by £27,000 you performed the calculations correctly but misinterpreted the result as an over absorption.

Chapter 6

Task 6.1

	Basis of apportionment	Silicon moulding £	Silicon extrusion £	Maintenance £	Stores £	General Admin £	Totals £
Depreciation of plant and equipment	NBV of plant and equipment	904,669	1,105,706				2,010,375
Power for production machinery	Production machinery power usage (KwH)	572,500	1,215,000				1,787,500
Rent and rates	Floor space			74,643	93,304	93,303	261,250
Light and heat	Floor space			16,500	20,625	20,625	57,750
Indirect labour	Allocated			253,750	90,125	600,250	944,125
Totals		1,477,169	2,320,706	344,893	204,054	714,178	5,061,000
Reapportion Maintenance		120,713	224,180	(344,893)			
Reapportion Stores		81,622	122,432		(204,054)		
Reapportion General Admin		357,089	357,089			(714,178)	
Total overheads to production centres		2,036,593	3,024,407				5,061,000

Task 6.2

(a)

	Basis of apportionment	Silicon moulding £	Silicon extrusion £	Maintenance £	Stores £	General Admin £	Totals £
Depreciation of plant and equipment	Headcount	972,762	1,037,613				2,010,375
Power for production machinery	Headcount	864,919	922,581				1,787,500
Rent and rates	Floor space			74,643	93,304	93,303	261,250
Light and heat	Floor space			16,500	20,625	20,625	57,750
Indirect labour	Allocated			253,750	90,125	600,250	944,125
Totals		1,837,681	1,960,194	344,893	204,054	714,178	5,061,000
Reapportion Maintenance		120,713	224,180	(344,893)			
Reapportion Stores		81,622	122,432		(204,054)		
Reapportion General Admin		464,216	249,962			(714,178)	
Total overheads to production centres		2,504,232	2,556,768				5,061,000

(b)

The manager would most likely argue with the revised basis of allocation as his costs have increased by £467,639. The use of headcount to apportion machinery costs is not common and the manager could argue that depreciation based on NBV, and power on consumption are better bases for reapportioning these costs. Nonetheless, if his cost centre is using more general admin then it is fair that he should bear more of that cost.

Chapter 7

Task 7.1

Service	Cost unit
Road, rail and air transport services	Passenger/kilometre, tonne/kilometre
Hotels	Occupied bed-night
Education	Full-time student
Hospitals	Patient-day
Catering establishments	Meal served

Task 7.2

Job number 03456

	Budget £	Actual £	Variance F/A £
Direct materials			
Plasterboard	3,600.00	3,500.00	100F
Wood & door frames	4,750.00	4,802.00	52A
Insulation	1,050.00	1,145.00	95A
Electrical fittings	320.00	300.00	20F
Windows	2,220.00	2,576.00	356A
Paint	270.00	250.00	20F
Direct labour			
Construction	554.00	641.00	87A
Electrical	224.00	160.00	64F
Decorating	165.00	205.00	40A
Direct expenses			
Hire of specialist lathe	240.00	240.00	0
Overheads (based upon direct labour hours)			
84/90 hours @ £15.00	1,260.00	1,350.00	90A

Task 7.3

(a) and (b)

	Budget £	Actual £	Variance F/A £	%
Direct materials				
Plasterboard	3,600.00	3,500.00	100F	2.8
Wood & door frames	4,750.00	4,802.00	52A	1.1
Insulation	1,050.00	1,145.00	95A	9.0
Electrical fittings	320.00	300.00	20F	6.3
Windows	2,220.00	2,576.00	356A	16.0
Paint	270.00	250.00	20F	7.4
Direct labour				
Construction	554.00	641.00	87A	15.7
Electrical	224.00	160.00	64F	28.6
Decorating	165.00	205.00	40A	24.2
Direct expenses				
Hire of specialist lathe	240.00	240.00	0	0
Overheads (based upon direct labour hours)				
84/90 hours @ £15.00	1,260.00	1,350.00	90A	7.1
Total cost	14,653.00	15,169.00	516.00 A	
Profit	2,930.60	2,414.60		
Net price	17,583.60	17,583.60		
VAT at 20%	3,516.72	3,516.72		
Total price	21,100.32	21,100.32		

(c) (2,930.60 − 2,414.60)/2,930.60 = 17.6%

Task 7.4

☑ High levels of indirect costs as a proportion of total cost

☑ Cost units are often intangible

☑ Use of composite cost units

In service costing it is difficult to identify many attributable direct costs. Many costs must be treated as indirect costs and shared over several cost units, therefore there are high levels of indirect costs as a proportion of total cost. Many services are intangible, for example a haircut or a cleaning service provide no physical, tangible product. Composite cost units such as passenger-mile or bed-night are often used in service costing. 'Use of equivalent units' does not apply because equivalent units are more often used in costing for tangible products.

Chapter 8

Task 8.1

(a)

Description	Kgs	Unit cost £	Total cost £	Description	Kgs	Unit cost £	Total cost £
Material TL4	700	1.35	945	Normal loss	73	0.70	51
Material TL3	350	1.50	525	Output	1,377	6.34	8,727
Material TL9	400	1.25	500				
Labour			3,700				
Overheads			3,108				
	1,450		8,778		1,450		8,778

(b)

	Debit	Credit
Abnormal loss account	✓	
Process account		✓

Task 8.2

Description	Kgs	Unit cost £	Total cost £	Description	Kgs	Unit cost £	Total cost £
Material TL4	700	1.35	945	Normal loss	145	0.70	102
Material TL3	350	1.50	525	Output	1,305	6.34	8,268
Material TL9	400	1.25	500				
Labour			3,040				
Overheads			3,360				
	1,450		8,370		1,450		8,370

The decision made to employ cheaper employees has resulted in the process costing more but higher losses are incurred too. However over time, the workers may get more efficient, taking less time and the losses may go down.

Task 8.3

The correct answer is 2,000 kg

Process account

	Dr		Cr
Opening WIP	4,500	Output	60,400
Input	54,300	Normal loss	400
Abnormal gain	2,000		-
	60,800		60,800

The abnormal gain is the balancing figure. 60,800 – 4,500 – 54,300 = 2,000

Task 8.4

The quantity of good production achieved was [2,625] kg.

Good production = input – normal loss – abnormal loss

$$= 3,000 - (10\% \times 3,000) - 75$$

$$= 3,000 - 300 - 75$$

$$= 2,625 \text{ kg}$$

Task 8.5

(a) The value credited to the process account for the scrap value of the normal loss for the period will be £ [100] (to the nearest £).

Normal loss = 10% × input

$$= 10\% \times 5,000 \text{ kg}$$

$$= 500 \text{ kg}$$

When scrap has a value, normal loss is valued at the value of the scrap ie 20p per kg.

Normal loss = £0.20 × 500 kg

$$= £100$$

(b) The amount of abnormal loss for the period is 300 kg.

	Kg
Input	5,000
Normal loss (10% × 5,000 kg)	(500)
Abnormal loss	(300)
Output	4,200

Chapter 9

Task 9.1

Batches produced and sold	3,000	3,750	5,000
	£	£	£
Sales revenue	60,000	75,000	100,000
Variable costs:			
• Direct materials 1.90	5,700	7,125	9,500
• Direct labour 9	27,000	33,750	45,000
• Overheads 3.1	9,300	11,625	15,500
Semi-variable costs: 2.70	9,450		
• Variable element		7,500	10,000
• Fixed element		3,450	3,450
Total cost	51,450	63,450	83,450
Total profit	8,550	11,550	16,550
Profit per batch (to 2 decimal places)	2.85	3.08	3.31

Task 9.2

(a) and (b)

Batches produced and sold	3,000	3,750	5,000
	£	£	£
Sales revenue	60,000	75,000	100,000
Variable costs:			
• Direct materials 2	6,000	7,500	10,000
• Direct labour 10	30,000	37,500	50,000
• Overheads 3.2	9,600	12,000	16,000
Semi-variable costs:	9,450		
• Variable element		7,500	10,000
• Fixed element		3,450	3,450
Total cost	55,050	67,950	89,450
Total profit	4,950	7,050	10,550
Profit per batch (to 2 decimal places)	1.65	1.88	2.11

Task 9.3

Batches produced and sold	3,000	4,000
	£	£
Sales revenue	60,000	80,000
Variable costs:		
• Direct materials	6,000	8,000
• Direct labour	30,000	40,000
• Overheads	9,600	12,800
Semi-variable costs:		
• Variable element	6,000	8,000
• Fixed element	3,450	3,450
Total cost	55,050	72,250
Total profit	4,950	7,750
Profit per batch (to 2 decimal places)	1.65	1.94

Reject.

The profit per batch is less than £2 at 4,000 batches, so management should reject the order.

....

Chapter 10

Task 10.1

	Flexed Budget	Actual	Variance	Favourable F or Adverse A
Volume sold	156,000	156,000		
	£'000	£'000	£'000	
Sales revenue	1,248	1,326	78	F
Less costs:				
Direct materials	390	372	18	F
Direct labour	468	444	24	F
Overheads	225	250	25	A
Operating profit	165	260	95	F

Task 10.2

	Flexed Budget	Actual	Budget unit cost/revenue	Actual unit cost/revenue
Volume sold	156,000	156,000		
	£'000	£'000		
Sales revenue	1,248	1,326	8	8.50
Less costs:				
Direct materials	390	372	2.50	2.38
Direct labour	468	444	3	2.85
Overheads	225	250		
Operating profit	165	260	1.06	1.67

They are all true. The unit selling price is higher than budgeted, which may be due to a rise in the sales price not planned for in the budget, or fewer bulk discounts to customers if these were planned for. The lower unit price for materials may arise from bulk buying discounts or new cheaper sources of supply. The lower labour costs may be due to a change in the make up of employees so there are more lower paid employees, or efficiency savings so fewer employees make the same number of SHEPs.

Chapter 11

Task 11.1

Production overheads absorbed into production	Debit: WIP	Credit: Production overheads
Indirect labour transferred to production overheads	Debit: Production overheads	Credit: Wages
Completed WIP transferred to finished goods	Debit: Finished goods	Credit: WIP
Direct materials issued to production	Debit: WIP	Credit: Materials

Task 11.2

	Drag and drop choice
Transaction 1	Debit: production overheads, Credit: income statement
Transaction 2	Debit: income statement, Credit: production overheads

Task 11.3

The correct answer is : Debit Production overhead control account Credit Materials control account

The cost of indirect materials issued is credited to the materials control account and 'collected' in the production overhead control account pending its absorption into work in progress.

Debit WIP account and Credit Materials control account represents the entries for the issue to production of **direct materials**.

Debit Cost of sales and Credit Materials control account is not correct. The issue of materials should not be charged direct to cost of sales. The cost of materials issued should first be analysed as direct or indirect and charged to work in progress or the overhead control account accordingly.

Chapter 12

Task 12.1

1 **(a)** **Absorption costing – unit cost**

	£
Direct materials	8.50
Direct labour	17.00
Variable overheads	3.00
Prime cost	28.50
Fixed overheads ((£850,000/250,000) × 2)	6.80
Absorption cost	35.30

(b) **Marginal costing – unit cost**

	£
Direct materials	8.50
Direct labour	17.00
Variable overheads	3.00
Prime cost or marginal cost	28.50

Task 12.2

In the long run, total profit for a company will be | the same for both types of costing | whether marginal costing or absorption costing is used.

Task 12.3

It might be argued that | absorption costing | is preferable **to** | marginal costing | **in management accounting,** in order to be consistent with the requirement of current accounting standards and financial reporting.

Task 12.4

(a) £45,400

		£	£
Sales	(5,200 × £30)		156,000
Direct materials	(5,800 × £6)	34,800	
Direct labour	(5,800 × £7.50)	43,500	
Variable overhead	(5,800 × £2.50)	14,500	
		92,800	
Less closing inventory	(600 × £16)	9,600	
			(83,200)
Contribution			72,800
Less fixed costs			27,400
			45,400

(b) £48,400

		£	£
Sales	(5,200 × £30)		156,000
Materials	(5,800 × £6)	34,800	
Labour	(5,800 × £7.50)	43,500	
Variable overhead	(5,800 × £2.50)	14,500	
Fixed costs	(5,800 × £5)	29,000	
Less closing inventories	(600 × £21)	(12,600)	
			(109,200)
Over-absorbed overhead (W)			1,600
Absorption costing profit			48,400

		£
Working		
Overhead absorbed	(5,800 x £5)	29,000
Overhead incurred		27,400
Over-absorbed overhead		1,600

Chapter 13

Task 13.1

(a) | 9,000 units |

(b) | £198,000 |

(c)

Units of COLIN sold	9,500	10,500
	£	£
Margin of safety (units)	500	1,500
Margin of safety percentage	5%	14%
Margin of safety revenue	11,000	33,000

(d) | 13,000 units |

(e) The correct answer is: the breakeven point will decrease and the margin of safety will increase

Task 13.2

(a) 8,000 x £(22-17) = £40,000

(b) | £132,000 | which is (£30,000/£5 x £22) or (6,000 × £22)

(c)

Units of COLIN sold	6,500	7,000
	£	£
Margin of safety (units)	500	1,000
Margin of safety percentage	8%	14%

(d) | 8,000 units | Yes as it is at the maximum level of production.

Task 13.3

The correct answer is 3,000 units

$$\text{Breakeven point } = \frac{\text{Fixed costs}}{\text{Contribution per unit}} = \frac{£30,000}{£(15-5)} = 3,000 \text{ units}$$

If you selected 2,000 units you divided the fixed cost by the selling price, but remember that the selling price also has to cover the variable cost. 4,000 units is the margin of safety, and if you selected 6,000 units, you divided the fixed cost by the variable cost per unit.

Task 13.4

The correct answer is: 20%

$$\text{Breakeven point } = \frac{\text{Fixed costs}}{\text{Contribution per unit}} = \frac{£96,000}{£(12-8)} = 24,000 \text{ units}$$

Budgeted sales   <u>30,000</u> units

Margin of safety   <u>6,000</u> units

$$\text{Expressed as a \% of budget } = \frac{6,000}{30,000} \times 100\% = 20\%$$

If you selected 25% you calculated the correct margin of safety in units, but you then expressed this as a percentage of the breakeven point. If you selected 73% you divided the fixed cost by the selling price to determine the breakeven point, but the selling price also has to cover the variable cost. You should have been able to eliminate 125% as an option; the margin of safety expressed as a percentage must always be less than 100 per cent.

Task 13.5

(a)   The correct answer is: 10,090 units

$$\text{Breakeven point } = \frac{\text{Fixed costs}}{\text{Contribution per unit}}$$

$$= \frac{10,000 \times £(4.00+0.80)}{(£6.00-(£1.20+£0.40))}$$

$$= \frac{£48,000}{£4.40} = 10,909 \text{ units}$$

If you selected 8,000 units you divided the fixed cost by the selling price, but the selling price also has to cover the variable cost. 8,333 units ignores the selling costs, but these are costs that must be covered before the breakeven point is reached. 10,000 units is the budgeted sales volume, which happens to be below the breakeven point.

(b) The correct answer is: 13,409 units

Contribution required for target profit	= fixed costs + profit
	= £48,000 + £11,000
	= £59,000
÷ Contribution per unit (from part (a))	= £4.40
∴ Sales units required	= 13,409 units

If you selected 2,500 units you divided the required profit by the contribution per unit, but the fixed costs must be covered before any profit can be earned. If you selected 9,833 units you identified correctly the contribution required for the target profit, but you then divided by the selling price per unit instead of the contribution per unit. 10,625 units ignores the selling costs, which must be covered before a profit can be earned.

....

Chapter 14

Task 14.1

(a) The net present value is **Negative**

	Year 0 £'000	Year 1 £'000	Year 2 £'000	Year 3 £'000	Year 4 £'000
Capital expenditure	(1,000)				
Sales income		350	400	400	350
Operating costs		(100)	(110)	(120)	(130)
Net cash flows	(1,000)	250	290	280	220
PV factors	1.0000	0.9009	0.8116	0.7312	0.6587
Discounted cash flows	(1,000)	225	235	205	145
Net present value	(190)				

(b) The payback period is **3** years and **10** months.

Task 14.2

£810,000. This is calculated as follows:

(all in £'000) 225 + 235 + 205 +145 – capital expenditure = 0

therefore capital expenditure = 810

Task 14.3

The net present value is **Positive**

	Year 0 £'000	Year 1 £'000	Year 2 £'000	Year 3 £'000	Year 4 £'000
Capital expenditure	(810)				
Sales income		350	400	400	350
Operating costs		(100)	(110)	(120)	(130)
Net cash flows	(810)	250	290	280	220
PV factors	1.0000	0.9346	0.8734	0.8163	0.7629
Discounted cash flows	(810)	234	253	229	168
Net present value	74				

Answer bank

AAT PRACTICE ASSESSMENT 1
COSTS AND REVENUES

Time allowed: 2½ hours

Section 1

Task 1.1

The inventory record shown below for plastic grade XL5 for the month of December has only been fully completed for the first three weeks of the month.

(a) **Complete the entries in the inventory record for the two receipts on 24 and 28 December.**

(b) **Complete ALL entries in the inventory record for the two issues in the month and for the closing balance at the end of December using the AVCO method of issuing inventory. Show the costs per kg in £ to three decimal places and the total costs in whole £.**

Inventory record for plastic grade XL5.

| Date | Receipts | | | Issues | | | Balance | |
	Quantity kg	Cost per kg (£)	Total cost (£)	Quantity kg	Cost per kg (£)	Total cost (£)	Quantity kg	Total cost (£)
Balance as at							100	119
24 December	500	1.298						
26 December				300				
28 December	500	1.304						
30 December				600				

The following forecast information is available for plastic grade XL5 for next year.

- Annual demand is 67,500 kilograms (kg).
- Annual holding cost per kg is £0.80.
- Fixed ordering cost is £1.20.

(c) **Calculate the Economic Order Quantity (EOQ) for XL5 for next year.**

[   ] kg

Task 1.2

Match the correct entries into the journal below to record the following FOUR accounting transactions:

Receipt of plastic components into inventory paying on credit. [ ]

Issue of plastic components from inventory to production. [ ]

Receipt of plastic components into inventory paying

immediately by BACS. [ ]

Return of plastic components from production to inventory. [ ]

| Debit: Bank
Credit: Inventory | Debit: Inventory, Credit
Purchase Ledger Control |

| Debit: Purchase Ledger
Control, Credit: Inventory | Debit: Inventory
Credit: Production |

| Debit: Inventory
Credit: Bank | Debit: Production
Credit: Inventory |

Task 1.3

Below is a weekly timesheet for one of Broadsword Ltd's employees, who is paid as follows:

- For a basic six-hour shift every day from Monday to Friday - basic pay.

- For any overtime in excess of the basic six hours, on any day from Monday to Friday - the extra hours are paid at time and a half (basic pay plus an overtime premium equal to half of basic pay).

- For three contracted hours each Saturday morning - basic pay.

- For any hours in excess of three hours on Saturday - the extra hours are paid at double time (basic pay plus an overtime premium equal to basic pay).

- For any hours worked on Sunday - paid at double time (basic pay plus an overtime premium equal to basic pay).

Complete the columns headed Basic pay, Overtime premium and Total pay in the table below.

(Notes: Zero figures should be entered in cells where appropriate. Overtime premium is just the premium paid for the extra hours worked.)

Employee's weekly timesheet for week ending 7 December

Employee: D Boy			Profit Centre: Plastic extrusion			
Employee Number: P450			Basic pay per hour: £ 12.00			
	Hours spent on production	Hours worked on indirect work	Notes	Basic pay £	Overtime premium £	Total pay £
Monday	6	2	10am-12pm Cleaning of machinery			
Tuesday	2	4	9am-1pm Customer care course			
Wednesday	8					
Thursday	6					
Friday	6	1	3-4pm Health and safety training			
Saturday	6					
Sunday	3					
Total	37	7				

Task 1.4

Broadsword Ltd's budgeted overheads for the next financial year are:

	£	£
Depreciation charge for plant and equipment		804,150
Power for production machinery		715,000
Rent and rates		104,500
Light and heat		23,100
Indirect labour costs:		
Maintenance	101,150	
Stores	36,050	
General Administration	240,100	
Total indirect labour cost		377,300

The following information is also available:

Department	Carrying amount of plant and equipment	Production machinery power usage (KwH)	Floor space (square metres)	Number of employees
Production centres:				
Plastic moulding	5,600,000	2,145,000		14
Plastic extrusion	2,400,000	1,430,000		10
Support cost centres:				
Maintenance			14,000	5
Stores			8,400	2
General Administration			5,600	7
Total	8,000,000	3,575,000	28,000	38

Overheads are allocated or apportioned on the most appropriate basis. The total overheads of the support cost centres are then reapportioned to the two production centres using the direct method.

- 76% of the Maintenance cost centre's time is spent maintaining production machinery in the Plastic moulding production centre and the remainder in the Plastic extrusion production centre.

- The Stores cost centre makes 60% of its issues to the Plastic moulding production centre, and 40% to the Plastic extrusion production centre.

- General Administration supports the two production centres equally.
- There is no reciprocal servicing between the three support cost centres.

Use the following table to allocate or apportion the overheads using the most appropriate basis.

	Basis of apportionment	Plastic moulding £	Plastic extrusion £	Maintenance £	Stores £	General Admin £	Total £
Depreciation charge for plant and equipment	▼						
Power for production machinery	▼						
Rent and rates	▼						
Light and heat	▼						
Indirect labour	▼						
Totals							
Reapportion Maintenance							
Reapportion Stores							
Reapportion General Admin							
Total overheads to production centres							

Picklist

Allocated
Carrying amount of plant and equipment
Floor Space
Production machinery power usage (KwH)

Task 1.5

Next quarter Broadsword Ltd's budgeted overheads and activity levels are:

	Plastic moulding	Plastic extrusion
Budgeted overheads (£)	325,996	178,200
Budgeted direct labour hours	16,300	9,900
Budgeted machine hours	5,258	3,300

(a) What would be the budgeted overhead absorption rate for each department, if this were set based on their both being heavily automated?

Plastic moulding £20/hour, Plastic extrusion £18/hour ☐

Plastic moulding £20/hour, Plastic extrusion £54/hour ☐

Plastic moulding £62/hour, Plastic extrusion £18/hour ☐

Plastic moulding £62/hour, Plastic extrusion £54/hour ☐

(b) What would be the budgeted overhead absorption rate for each department, if this were set based on their both being labour intensive?

Plastic moulding £20/hour, Plastic extrusion £18/hour ☐

Plastic moulding £20/hour, Plastic extrusion £54/hour ☐

Plastic moulding £62/hour, Plastic extrusion £18/hour ☐

Plastic moulding £62/hour, Plastic extrusion £54/hour ☐

At the end of the quarter actual overheads incurred were found to be:

	Plastic moulding	Plastic extrusion
Actual overheads	315,906	198,100

(c) Assuming that exactly the same amount of overheads was absorbed as budgeted, what were the budgeted under or over absoptions in the quarter?

Plastic moulding over absorbed £10,090, Plastic extrusion over absorbed £19,900 ☐

Plastic moulding over absorbed £10,090, Plastic extrusion under absorbed £19,900 ☐

Plastic moulding under absorbed £10,090, Plastic extrusion under absorbed £19,900 ☐

Plastic moulding under absorbed £10,090, Plastic extrusion over absorbed £19,900 ☐

Section 2

Task 2.1

Broadsword Ltd has prepared a forecast for the next quarter for one of its small plastic components, ZY24. This component is produced in batches and the forecast is based on selling and producing 1,200 batches. One of the customers of Broadsword Ltd has indicated that it may be significantly increasing its order level for component ZY24 for the next quarter and it appears that activity levels of 1,500 batches and 2,000 batches are feasible.

The semi-variable costs should be calculated using the high-low method. If 3,000 batches are sold, the total semi-variable cost will be £7,380, and there is a constant unit variable cost up to this volume.

Complete the table below and calculate the estimated profit per batch of ZY24 at the different activity levels.

Batches produced and sold	1,200	1,500	2,000
	£	£	£
Sales revenue	36,000		
Variable costs			
Direct costs	5,400		
Direct labour	12,600		
Overheads	7,200		
Semi-variable costs	3,780		
Variable element			
Fixed element			
Total cost	28,980		
Total profit	7,020		
Profit per batch (to 2 decimal places)	5.85		

Task 2.2

The product TR28 has a selling price of £23 per unit with a total variable cost of £15 per unit. Broadsword Ltd estimates that the fixed costs per quarter associated with this product are £36,000.

(a) Calculate the budgeted breakeven, in units, for product TR28.

| | units

(b) Calculate the budgeted breakeven, in £s, for product TR28

£ | |

(c) Complete the table below to show the budgeted margin of safety in units and the margin of safety percentage if Broadsword Ltd sells 5,000 or 6,000 units of product TR28.

	5,000	6,000
Margin of safety (units)	units	units
Margin of safety percentage	%	%

(d) If Broadsword Ltd wishes to make a profit of £20,000, how many units of TR28 must it sell?

| | units

(e) If Broadsword Ltd increases the selling price of TR28 by £1, what will be the impact on the breakeven point and the margin of safety, assuming no change in the number of units sold?

The breakeven point will decrease and the margin of safety will increase. ☐

The breakeven point will stay the same but the margin of safety will decrease. ☐

The breakeven point will decrease and the margin of safety will stay the same. ☐

The breakeven point will increase and the margin of safety will decrease. ☐

Task 2.3

The Plastic extrusion department of Broadsword Ltd uses process costing for some of its products.

The process account for December for one particular process has been partly completed but the following information is also relevant:

Two employees worked on this process during December. Each employee worked 40 hours per week for 4 weeks and was paid £10 per hour.

Overheads are absorbed on the basis of £16 per labour hour.

Broadsword Ltd expects a normal loss of 5% during this process, which it then sells for scrap at 60p per kg.

(a) Complete the process account below for December.

Description	Kg	Unit cost £	Total cost £	Description	Kg	Unit cost £	Total cost £
Material XG4	600	1.20		Normal Loss		0.60	
Material XH3	400	1.50		Output	1330		
Material XJ9	400	0.61					
Labour							
Overheads							

(b) Identify the correct entry for each of the following in a process account.

Abnormal loss [▼]

Abnormal gain [▼]

Picklist

Debit
Credit

Task 2.4

Broadsword has the following original budget and actual performance for product ZT4 for the year ending 31 December.

	Budget	Actual
Volume sold	100,000	144,000
	£'000	£'000
Sales revenue	2,000	3,600
Less costs:		
Direct materials	350	530
Direct labour	400	480
Overheads	980	1,228
Profit from operations	270	1,362

Both direct materials and direct labour are variable costs. The overheads are fixed up to a volume of 120,000 units and then increase to £1,228,000.

Complete the table below to show a flexed budget and the resulting variances against this budget for the year. Show the actual variance amount, for sales and each cost, in the column headed 'variance' and indicate whether this is Favourable or Adverse by entering F or A in the final column, if neither F nor A enter 0.

	Flexed budget	Actual	Variance	Favourable F, Adverse A Neither 0
Volume sold		144,000		
	£'000	£'000	£'000	
Sales revenue		3,600		
Less costs:				
Direct materials		530		
Direct labour		480		
Overheads		1,228		
Profit from operations		1,362		

Task 2.5

One of the extrusion machines in the Plastic extrusion department is nearing the end of its useful life and Broadsword Ltd is considering purchasing a replacement machine.

Estimates have been made for the initial capital cost, sales revenue and operating costs of the replacement machine, which is expected to have a useful life of three years:

	Year 0 £'000	Year 1 £'000	Year 2 £'000	Year 3 £'000
Capital expenditure	900			
Other cash flows				
Sales revenue		420	560	800
Operating costs		120	150	190

The company appraises capital investment projects using a 15% cost of capital.

(a) **Complete the table below and calculate the net present value of the proposed replacement machine (to the nearest £'000). You MUST indicate negative numbers where appropriate in order to obtain full marks.**

	Year 0 £'000	Year 1 £'000	Year 2 £'000	Year 3 £'000
Capital expenditure				
Sales revenue				
Operating costs				
Net cash flows				
PV factors	1.000	0.8696	0.7561	0.6575
Discounted cash flows				
Net present value				

The net present value is [   ]

Options: positive / negative

....

(b) **Calculate the payback period of the replacement machine to the nearest whole month.**

The payback period is [   ] years and [   ] months.

....

AAT PRACTICE ASSESSMENT 1
COSTS AND REVENUES

ANSWERS

Section 1

Task 1.1

(a) + (b)   Inventory record for plastic grade XL5.

Date	Receipts Quantity kg	Receipts Cost per kg (£)	Receipts Total cost (£)	Issues Quantity kg	Issues Cost per kg (£)	Issues Total cost (£)	Balance Quantity kg	Balance Total cost (£)
Balance as at							100	119
24 December	500	1.298	649				600	768
26 December				300	1.280	384	300	384
28 December	500	1.304	652				800	1,036
30 December				600	1.295	777	200	259

(c) | 450 | kg

. . . .

Task 1.2

Receipt of plastic components into inventory paying on credit.

Debit: Inventory, Credit: Purchase Ledger Control

Issue of plastic components from inventory to production.

Debit: Production
Credit: Inventory

Receipt of plastic components into inventory paying immediately by BACS.

Debit: Inventory
Credit: Bank

Return of plastic components from production to inventory.

Debit: Inventory
Credit: Production

Debit: Bank
Credit: Inventory

Debit: Purchase Ledger Control, Credit: Inventory

. . . .

Task 1.3

Employee's weekly timesheet for week ending in 7 December

Employee: D Boy			Profit Centre: Plastic extrusion			
Employee Number: P450			Basic pay per hour: £ 12.00			
	Hours spent on production	Hours worked on indirect work	Notes	Basic pay £	Overtime premium £	Total pay £
Monday	6	2	10am-12pm Cleaning of machinery	96	12	108
Tuesday	2	4	9am-1pm Customer care course	72	0	72
Wednesday	8			96	12	108
Thursday	6			72	0	72
Friday	6	1	3-4pm Health and safety training	84	6	90
Saturday	6			72	36	108
Sunday	3			0	72	72
Total	37	7		492	138	630

Sunday hours

The figures for Sunday hours in this task may be entered as 3 hours of double time made up of either:

- £0 basic pay and £72 overtime premium, viewing all of the hours on Sunday as overtime premium (as shown in the model answer); or

- £36 basic pay plus £36 overtime premium.

Both methods are equally valid for the purposes of this assessment. Please note that the figures in the total row will need to be duly adjusted if using the second method.

Task 1.4

	Basis of apportionment	Plastic moulding £	Plastic extrusion £	Maintenance £	Stores £	General Admin £	Totals £
Depreciation charge for plant and equipment	Carrying amount of plant and equipment	562,905	241,245				804,150
Power for production machinery	Production machinery power usage (KwH)	429,000	286,000				715,000
Rent and rates	Floor space			52,250	31,350	20,900	104,500
Light and heat	Floor space			11,550	6,930	4,620	23,100
Indirect labour	Allocated			101,150	36,050	240,100	377,300
Totals		991,905	527,245	164,950	74,330	265,620	2,024,050
Reapportion Maintenance		125,362	39,588	(164,950)			
Reapportion Stores		44,598	29,732		(74,330)		
Reapportion General Admin		132,810	132,810			(265,620)	
Total overheads to production centres		1,294,675	729,375				2,024,050

Task 1.5

(a)

Plastic moulding £20/hour, Plastic extrusion £18/hour	☐
Plastic moulding £20/hour, Plastic extrusion £54/hour	☐
Plastic moulding £62/hour, Plastic extrusion £18/hour	☐
Plastic moulding £62/hour, Plastic extrusion £54/hour	☑

(b)

Plastic moulding £20/hour, Plastic extrusion £18/hour	☑
Plastic moulding £20/hour, Plastic extrusion £54/hour	☐
Plastic moulding £62/hour, Plastic extrusion £18/hour	☐
Plastic moulding £62/hour, Plastic extrusion £54/hour	☐

(c)

Plastic moulding over absorbed £10,090, Plastic extrusion over absorbed £19,900	☐
Plastic moulding over absorbed £10,090, Plastic extrusion under absorbed £19,900	☑
Plastic moulding under absorbed £10,090, Plastic extrusion under absorbed £19,900	☐
Plastic moulding under absorbed £10,090, Plastic extrusion over absorbed £19,900	☐

Section 2

Task 2.1

Batches produced and sold	1,200	1,500	2,000
	£	£	£
Sales revenue	36,000	45,000	60,000
Variable costs			
Direct costs	5,400	6,750	9,000
Direct labour	12,600	15,750	21,000
Overheads	7,200	9,000	12,000
Semi-variable costs	3,780		
Variable element		3,000	4,000
Fixed element		1,380	1,380
Total cost	28,980	35,880	47,380
Total profit	7,020	9,120	12,620
Profit per batch (to 2 decimal places)	5.85	6.08	6.31

Task 2.2

(a)

| 4,500 | units |

(b)

£ | 103,500 |

(c)

	5,000		6,000	
Margin of safety (units)	500	units	1,500	units
Margin of safety percentage	10	%	25	%

(d)

| 7,000 | units |

(e)

The breakeven point will decrease and the margin of safety will increase.	✓
The breakeven point will stay the same but the margin of safety will decrease.	☐
The breakeven point will decrease and the margin of safety will stay the same.	☐
The breakeven point will increase and the margin of safety will decrease.	☐

Task 2.3

(a)

Description	Kg	Unit cost £	Total cost £	Description	Kg	Unit cost £	Total cost £
Material XG4	600	1.20	720	Normal Loss	70	0.60	42
Material XH3	400	1.50	600	Output	1,330	7.40	9,842
Material XJ9	400	0.61	244				
Labour			3,200				
Overheads			5,120				
	1,400		9,884		1,400		9,884

(b)

Abnormal loss	Credit
Abnormal gain	Debit

Task 2.4

	Flexed budget	Actual	Variance	Favourable F, Adverse A Neither 0
Volume sold	144,000	144,000		
	£'000	£'000	£'000	
Sales revenue	2,880	3,600	720	F
Less costs:				
Direct materials	504	530	26	A
Direct labour	576	480	96	F
Overheads	980	1,228	248	A
Profit from operations	820	1,362	542	F

Task 2.5

(a)

	Year 0 £'000	Year 1 £'000	Year 2 £'000	Year 3 £'000
Capital expenditure	(900)			
Sales revenue		420	560	800
Operating costs		(120)	(150)	(190)
Net cash flows	(900)	300	410	610
PV factors	1.000	0.8696	0.7561	0.6575
Discounted cash flows	(900)	261	310	401
Net present value	72			

The net present value is   Positive

··

(b)

The payback period is [2] years and [4] months.

··

AAT PRACTICE ASSESSMENT 2
COSTS AND REVENUES

Time allowed: 2½ hours

Section 1

Task 1.1

Broadsword Ltd uses raw material TY6 in the manufacture of its products. Issues to production are valued using the first in first out basis (FIFO).

The partially completed inventory record for December for TY6 is shown below.

(a) **Complete ALL entries in the inventory record for the receipts and issues of TY6 during December, showing the closing balance at 31 December. Cost per kilogram entries should be completed in £ to THREE decimal places. (Note: Only one entry is permitted per inventory record cell.)**

Inventory record for TY6

Date	Receipts			Issues			Balance	
	Quantity kg	Cost per kg (£)	Total cost (£)	Quantity kg	Cost per kg (£)	Total cost (£)	Quantity kg	Total cost (£)
Balance 1 December							10,000	30,000
3 December	20,000		62,000					
14 December				10,000				
19 December	14,000	3.05						
31 December				10,000				

Broadsword could have valued issues to production using the weighted average cost method (AVCO).

(b) **Select the total cost of the balance of inventory remaining after the issue of inventory on 14 December if valued using the weighted average cost method.**

£3.07 ☐

£61,333.33 ☐

£62,000 ☐

£30,667 ☐

Task 1.2

In December Broadsword Ltd made a number of transactions which must be accounted for using the journal.

The following codes are relevant:

Code	Account name
2084	Grade 84 plastic
2839	H52839 component
3767	DV67 work in progress
4000	Bank
4500	Purchase ledger control

(a) **Identify the correct entries in the journal to record the transaction by inserting the appropriate options in the relevant boxes, and inserting the correct amounts (correct to TWO decimal places).**

Receipt of 10kg Grade 84 plastic into inventory as a cash purchase at £15/kg.

	Account code	Account name	Amount £
Debit			
Credit			

Options for (a):

| 2,084 | 2,839 | 3,767 | 4,000 | 4,500 |

| Bank | Purchase ledger control | DV67 work in progress |

| Grade 84 plastic | H52839 component |

(b) Identify the correct entries in the journal to record the transaction by inserting the appropriate options in the relevant boxes, and inserting the correct amounts (correct to TWO decimal places).

Issue of 17 units of type H52839 component (cost £408 per 50 units) to production of DV67.

	Account code	Account name	Amount £
Debit			
Credit			

Options for (b):

| 2,084 | 2,839 | 3,767 | 4,000 | 4,500 |

| Bank | Purchase ledger control | DV67 work in progress |

| Grade 84 plastic | H52839 component |

··

Five units of H52839 component were not used in production of 'DV67 work in progress' and were returned to inventory.

(c) Complete the following sentence by selecting appropriate items from each picklist.

To account for this, account 3767 should be [▼] and account 2839 should be [▼]

Picklist

Debited
Credited

··

Task 1.3

Broadsword Ltd pays its employees on a weekly basis. All employees are required to complete a weekly timesheet which is then used to calculate the gross pay due. Basic pay is calculated as total hours worked multiplied by the basic rate.

Complete the timesheet below using the data below. (Note: Overtime premium is just the premium paid for the extra hours worked. Your figures should be entered to two decimal places. If no hours are due then you must enter a zero figure in the relevant table cell.)

Employee: J. Bains			Profit Centre: Plastic extrusion			
Employee Number: P201			Basic pay per hour: £ 11.00			
	Hours spent on production	Hours worked on indirect work	Notes	Basic pay £	Overtime premium £	Total pay £
Monday	8					
Tuesday	5	3	Training course 8am-11am			
Wednesday	7					
Thursday	9					
Friday	6	2	Inventory check briefing 2pm-4pm			
Saturday		6	Inventory checking			
Sunday		4	Inventory checking			
Total	35	15				

Data

- The timesheet is for J. Bains, an employee in the Plastic extrusion department for the week ended 14 December. Employees in the Plastic extrusion department are paid as follows:

  - For a basic seven-hour shift every day from Monday to Friday, and three hours on a Saturday - £11 per hour.

  - For any overtime in excess of the seven hours, on any day from Monday to Friday – the additional hours are paid at basic pay plus an overtime premium equal to half of the basic pay (time and a half).

  - For any overtime in excess of the three contracted hours on a Saturday - the additional hours are paid at basic pay plus an overtime premium equal to basic pay (double time).

  - Any hours worked on Sunday are paid at basic rate plus an overtime premium equal to basic pay (double time).

Task 1.4

Broadsword Ltd is preparing its budgets for the first quarter of next year. The Chief Accountant has estimated overhead expenses as: Depreciation charge for plant and equipment £562,400, Power £298,500, Rent and rates £64,000, and Light and heat £28,600. In addition, he has provided the following information:

Department	Carrying amount of machinery (£)	Machinery power usage (KwH)	Floor space (square metres)	Number of employees	Indirect labour cost (£)
Production centres:					
Plastic moulding	4,902,400	330,000	12,000	20	
Plastic extrusion	2,757,600	270,000	12,000	14	
Support cost centres:					
Maintenance			2,700	10	98,206
Stores			1,500	2	21,070
General Administration			1,800	5	39,850
Total	7,660,000	600,000	30,000	51	159,126

Overheads are allocated or apportioned using the most appropriate basis. The total overheads of the support cost centres are then reapportioned to the two production centres using the direct method.

- 65% of the Maintenance cost centre's time is spent maintaining production machinery in the Plastic moulding production centre, and the remainder in the Plastic extrusion production centre.

- The Stores cost centre makes 40% of its issues to the Plastic moulding production centre, and 60% to the Plastic extrusion production centre.

- General Administration supports the two production centres equally.

- There is no reciprocal servicing between the three support cost centres.

Use the following table to allocate or apportion the overheads using the most appropriate basis.

	Basis of apportionment	Plastic moulding £	Plastic extrusion £	Maintenance £	Stores £	General Admin £	Totals £
Depreciation charge for machinery	▼						
Power for production	▼						
Rent and rates	▼						
Light and heat	▼						
Indirect labour	▼						
Totals							
Reapportion Maintenance							
Reapportion Stores							
Reapportion General Admin							
Total overheads to production centres							

Picklist

Allocated
Carrying amount of machinery
Floor Space
Number of employees
Production machinery power usage (KwH)

Task 1.5

The following information is available for the Plastic moulding and Plastic extrusion departments.

Quarter 1	Plastic moulding	Plastic extrusion
Budgeted direct labour hours	4,150	4,900
Budgeted machine hours	3,500	5,220
Actual direct labour hours	4,250	5,000
Actual machine hours	3,400	5,100
Budgeted overheads	£93,375	£225,765
Actual overheads	£96,500	£215,400

(a) The budgeted overhead absorption rate (to TWO decimal places) for the Plastic moulding department based upon labour hours and for the Plastic extrusion department based upon machine hours, is:

	Plastic moulding £	Plastic extrusion £
Budgeted overhead absorption rate		per hour		per hour

(b) If the overhead absorption rate for the Plastic extrusion is £44 per machine hour, the actual overheads incurred were £250,000 and the actual machine hours used were 5,900 hours, complete the following table:

	Overheads incurred £	Overheads absorbed £	Under/over absorption £	Under/over absorption?
Plastic extrusion department				▼

(c) Complete the following sentence by selecting the appropriate response and inserting the correct amount:

In Quarter 1 overheads for the Plastic moulding department were [▼] by:

£ [   ]

Picklist

Under-absorbed
Over-absorbed

Section 2

Task 2.1

Broadsword Ltd has prepared a forecast for the next month for one of its products, LT92.

The forecast is based on selling and producing 750 batches.

One of Broadsword Ltd's customers has indicated that it may be significantly increasing its order level for product LT92, so it now appears that activity levels of 1,250 batches and 2,250 batches are feasible.

The fixed costs are fixed within a production range of up to 2,500 batches. Above that level extra indirect labour costs will be incurred.

(a) Complete the table below and calculate the estimated profit per batch of LT92 at the different activity levels.

LT92 batches produced and sold	750	1,250	2,250
	£	£	£
Sales revenue	11250		
Variable costs:			
• Direct materials	3750		
• Direct labour	2250		
• Overheads	1125		
Fixed costs:			
• Indirect labour	1750		
• Overheads	500		
Total cost	9375		
Total profit	1875		
Profit per batch (to 2 decimal places)	2.50		

Broadsword Ltd estimates that if it produced 2,500 batches of LT92 there will be extra fixed costs of £750.

(b) Complete the following sentences by using the picklists and inserting an amount (correct to TWO decimal places).

The profit per batch of LT92 increases with increasing activity levels up to 2,500 batches

because [▼]

Picklist

Variable costs per batch decrease
Variable costs per batch increase
Fixed costs per batch increase
Fixes costs per batch decrease

With extra fixed costs of £750 the profit per batch at a production level of 2,500 batches

will [▼] by £ [   ]

Picklist

Increase
Decrease

....

Task 2.2

Broadsword Ltd has prepared annual budgeted information for two of its products, AZ10 and BY29.

Product	AZ10	BY29	Total
Units sold	50,000	30,000	80,000
Sales revenue (£)	75,000	52,500	127,500
Direct materials (£)	20,000	15,000	35,000
Direct labour (£)	30,000	21,000	51,000
Variable overheads (£)	5,000	6,000	11,000
Fixed overheads (£)	15,000	16,000	31,000

(a) **Complete the table below (to two decimal places) to show the budgeted contribution per unit of AZ10 and BY29 sold, and the company's budgeted profit or loss for the year from these two products.**

	AZ10 (£)	BY29 (£)	Total (£)
Selling price per unit			
Less: variable costs per unit			
Direct material			
Direct labour			
Variable overheads			
Contribution per unit			
Sales volume (units)			
Total contribution			
Less: fixed costs			31,000
Budgeted ▼			

Picklist

Profit
Loss

The total cost of producing 2,200 units of PD66 has been calculated as £17,000 and of producing 3,500 units is £22,200. The only increase in cost is the increased volume of production.

(b) **Complete the following sentence by entering the appropriate figure (to 2 decimal places).**

The fixed cost of producing PD66 is £ [   ] and the variable cost of

producing one unit of PD66 is: £ [   ] .

Task 2.3

Broadsword Ltd is to begin producing a new plastic component as from 1 January. It will be using process costing to account for the manufacture of this new component.

The component requires the input of three different materials:

Material 1 - 200 kilograms @ £12.00 per kilogram

Material 2 - 600 kilograms @ £10.00 per kilogram

Material 3 - 200 kilograms @ £4.00 per kilogram.

(a) **Complete the table below (to two decimal places) to show the total cost of the materials input into the process.**

Materials	£
Material 1	
Material 2	
Material 3	
Total	

Broadsword estimates that the process will require three operatives to work 25 hours each. These operatives will be paid an hourly rate of £8.

Overheads are to be absorbed on the basis of £24 per direct labour hour.

(b) **Calculate the total labour cost and total overhead cost for the manufacture of the new plastic component, to two decimal places, and complete the sentences below.**

The total labour cost for the manufacture of the new plastic component is: £ [   ]

The total overhead cost for the manufacture of the new plastic component is: £ [   ]

(c) **Calculate the total quantity and value of inputs into the process for the new plastic component, to two decimal places, and complete the sentence below.**

The total quantity of materials input into the process is: [   ] kilograms, and

the total value of inputs into the process is: £ [   ] .

Broadsword expects 15% of the input to be scrapped during the manufacturing process. The scrap can be sold at £3.78 per kilogram.

(d) **Calculate the total scrap value of the normal loss of 15% of input. Your answer must be stated to two decimal places.**

The total scrap value of the normal loss of 15% of input is £ [   ]

(e) **Calculate the cost per kilogram of output assuming a normal loss of 15% of input. Your answer must be stated to four decimal places.**

The cost per kilogram of output assuming a normal loss of 15% of input is

£ [   ]

(f)   Complete the sentences below, using the picklist and gapfill, to identify the appropriate accounting entries. Enter your answers to two decimal places.

If the process results in an output of 865 kilograms there will be [▼] of

[   ] kilograms. This will have a total value of £ [   ] .

Picklist

An abnormal loss
A normal loss
An abnormal gain
A normal gain

Task 2.4

Broadsword Ltd budgeted to manufacture 12,000 units of product PD72 last quarter. The budgeted and actual results for the quarter were as follows:

	Budget	Actual
Number of units	12,000	14,000
	£	£
Sales revenue	180,000	215,200
Less costs:		
Direct materials	38,400	43,400
Direct labour	69,600	83,300
Fixed overheads	40,000	41,250
Profit from operations	32,000	47,250

All operating costs are variable except the fixed overheads.

Complete the table below to show a flexed budget and the resulting variances against this budget for the quarter. Show the actual variance amount, for sales and each cost, in the column headed 'Variance'. Adverse variances must be denoted with a minus sign. Enter 0 where any figure is zero.

	Flexed budget	Actual	Variance
Number of units		14,000	
	£	£	£
Sales revenue		215,200	
Less costs:			
Direct materials		43,400	
Direct labour		83,300	
Fixed overheads		41,250	
Profit from operations		47,250	

Task 2.5

Broadsword Ltd is considering replacing one of the moulding machines in the Plastic moulding department because it has become unreliable and repairs are proving to be expensive.

The following estimates of initial capital cost, sales income and operating costs of one possible replacement machine have been obtained. The estimated useful life of this moulding machine is three years.

	Year 0 £'000	Year 1 £'000	Year 2 £'000	Year 3 £'000
Capital expenditure	600			
Other cash flows:				
Sales income		280	350	450
Operating costs		110	140	160

Broadsword appraises capital investment projects using a cost of capital of 15%.

(a) **Complete the table below to calculate the net present value of the proposed replacement machine (to the nearest £'000). Use a minus sign to indicate a negative figure. Enter 0 where any figure is zero.**

	Year 0 £'000	Year 1 £'000	Year 2 £'000	Year 3 £'000
Capital expenditure				
Sales income				
Operating costs				
Net cash flows				
PV factors	1.0000	0.8696	0.7561	0.6575
Discounted cash flows				
Net present value				

(b) **Identify whether the net present value of the proposed replacement machine is positive or negative.**

The net present value is [▼]

Picklist

Negative
Positive

(c) Calculate the payback of the possible replacement moulding machine in years and months. Enter whole numbers only. Partial months must be rounded up to the next month.

The payback period is [   ] years and [   ] months.

AAT PRACTICE ASSESSMENT 2
COSTS AND REVENUES

ANSWERS

Section 1

Task 1.1

(a)

Inventory record for TY6

Date	Receipts			Issues			Balance	
	Quantity kg	Cost per kg (£)	Total cost (£)	Quantity kg	Cost per kg (£)	Total cost (£)	Quantity kg	Total cost (£)
Balance 1 December							10,000	30,000
3 December	20,000	3.1	62,000				30,000	92,000
14 December				10,000	3	30,000	20,000	62,000
19 December	14,000	3.05	42,700				34,000	104,700
31 December				10,000	3.1	31,000	24,000	73,700

(b)

£3.07	☐
£61,333.33	☑
£62,000	☐
£30,667	☐

Task 1.2

(a)

Receipt of 10 kg Grade 84 plastic into inventory as cash purchase at £15/kg.

	Account code	Account name	Amount £
Debit	2,084	Grade 84 plastic	150
Credit	4,000	Bank	150

(b)

Issue of 17 units of type H52839 component (cost £408 per 50 units) to production of DV67.

	Account code	Account name	Amount £
Debit	3767	DV67 work in progress	138.72
Credit	2839	H52839 component	138.72

(c)

To account for this, account 3767 should be credited and account 2839 should be debited.

Task 1.3

Employee: J. Bains			Profit Centre: Plastic extrusion		
Employee Number: P201			Basic pay per hour: £ 11.00		
	Hours spent on production	Hours worked on indirect work	Notes	Basic pay £	Overtime premium £	Total pay £
Monday	8			88	5.5	93.5
Tuesday	5	3	Training course 8am-11am	88	5.5	93.5
Wednesday	7			77	0	77
Thursday	9			99	11	110
Friday	6	2	Stock take briefing 2pm-4pm	88	5.5	93.5
Saturday		6	Stock taking	66	33	99
Sunday		4	Stock taking	44	44	88
Total	35	15		550	104.5	654.5

Sunday hours

The figures for Sunday hours in this task may be entered as 4 hours of double time made up of either:

- £44 basic pay plus £44 overtime premium (as shown in the model answer); or

- £0 basic pay and £88 overtime premium, viewing all of the hours on Sunday as overtime premium.

Both methods are equally valid for the purposes of this assessment. Please note that the figures in the total row will need to be duly adjusted if using the second method.

Task 1.4

	Basis of apportion ment	Plastic moulding £	Plastic extrusion £	Maintenance £	Stores £	General Admin £	Totals £
Depreciation charge for machinery	Carrying amount of machinery	359,936	202,464				562,400
Power for production	Production machinery power usage (KwH)	164,175	134,325				298,500
Rent and rates	Floor space	25,600	25,600	5,760	3,200	3840	64,000
Light and heat	Floor space	11,440	11,440	2,574	1,430	1,716	28,600
Indirect labour	Allocated			98,206	21,070	39,850	159,126
Totals		561,151	373,829	106,540	25,700	45,406	1,112,626
Reapportion Maintenance		69,251	37,289	106,540			
Reapportion stores		10,280	15,420		25,700		
Reapportion General Admin		22,703	22,703			45,406	
Total overheads to production centres		663,385	449,241				1,112,626

Task 1.5

(a)

	Plastic moulding £		Plastic extrusion £	
Budgeted overhead absorption rate	22.5	per hour	43.25	per hour

(b)

	Overheads incurred £	Overheads absorbed £	Under/over absorption £	Under/over absorption?
Plastic extrusion department	250,000	259,600	9,600	over

(c)

In Quarter 1 overheads for the Plastic moulding department were under-absorbed by:

£ 875

Section 2

Task 2.1

(a)

LT92 batches produced and sold	750	1,250	2,250
	£	£	£
Sales revenue	11,250	18,750	33,750
Variable costs:			
• Direct materials	3,750	6,250	11,250
• Direct labour	2,250	3,750	6,750
• Overheads	1,125	1,875	3,375
Fixed costs:			
• Indirect labour	1,750	1,750	1,750
• Overheads	500	500	500
Total cost	9,375	14,125	23,625
Total profit	1,875	4,625	10,125
Profit per batch (to 2 decimal places)	2.50	3.7	4.5

(b)

The profit per batch of LT92 increases with increasing activity levels up to 2,500 batches because | fixed costs per batch decrease. |

With extra fixed costs of £750 the profit per batch at a production level of 2,500 batches will | decrease | by £ | 0.30 |

Task 2.2

(a)

	AZ10 (£)	BY29 (£)	Total (£)
Selling price per unit	1.5	1.75	
Less: variable costs per unit			
Direct material	0.4	0.5	
Direct labour	0.6	0.7	
Variable overheads	0.1	0.2	
Contribution per unit	0.4	0.35	
Sales volume (units)	50,000	30,000	
Total contribution	20,000	10,500	30,500
Less: fixed costs			31,000
Budgeted loss			500

(b)

The fixed cost of producing PD66 is £ 8,200 and the variable cost of producing

one unit of PD66 is: £ 4

Task 2.3

(a)

Materials	£
Material 1	2,400
Material 2	6,000
Material 3	800
Total	9,200

(b)

The total labour cost for the manufacture of the new plastic component is: £ 600

The total overhead cost for the manufacture of the new plastic component is: £ 1,800

(c)

The total quantity of materials input into the process is: 1,000 kilograms, and

the total value of inputs into the process is: £ 11,600 .

(d)

The total scrap value of the normal loss of 15% of input is £ 567

(e)

The cost per kilogram of output assuming a normal loss of 15% of input is

£ 12.98

....

(f)

If the process results in an output of 865 kilograms there will be an abnormal gain of

15 kilograms. This will have a total value of £ 194.7 .

....

Task 2.4

	Flexed budget	Actual	Variance
Number of units	14,000	14,000	
	£	£	£
Sales revenue	210,000	215,200	5,200
Less costs:			
Direct materials	44,800	43,400	1,400
Direct labour	81,200	83,300	(2,100)
Fixed overheads	40,000	41,250	(1,250)
Profit from operations	44,000	47,250	3,250

....

Task 2.5

(a)

	Year 0 £'000	Year 1 £'000	Year 2 £'000	Year 3 £'000
Capital expenditure	(600)			
Sales income		280	350	450
Operating costs		(110)	(140)	(160)
Net cash flows	(600)	170	210	290
PV factors	1.0000	0.8696	0.7561	0.6575
Discounted cash flows	(600)	148	159	191
Net present value	(103)			

(b)

The net present value is negative

(c)

The payback period is [2] years and [10] months.

BPP PRACTICE ASSESSMENT 1
COSTS AND REVENUES

Time allowed: 2½ hours

Costs and Revenues BPP practice assessment 1

Section 1

Task 1.1

The following information is available for fibreglass panels:

- Annual demand 156,250 kilograms
- Annual holding cost per kilogram £2.50
- Fixed ordering cost £5

(a) **Calculate the Economic Order Quantity (EOQ) for fibreglass panels.**

The inventory record shown below for plastic grade FIBREGLASS PANELS for the month of July has only been fully completed for the first three weeks of the month.

(b) **Complete the entries in the inventory record for the two receipts on 24 and 28 July that were ordered using the EOQ method.**

(c) **Complete ALL entries in the inventory record for the two issues in the month and for the closing balance at the end of July, using the AVCO method of issuing inventory.**

(Show the costs per kilogram (kg.) in £s to 3 decimal places; and the total costs in whole £s).

Inventory record for plastic grade FIBREGLASS PANELS

Date	Receipts			Issues			Balance	
	Quantity kgs	Cost per kg (£)	Total cost (£)	Quantity kgs	Cost per kg (£)	Total cost (£)	Quantity kgs	Total cost (£)
Balance as at 22 July							120	276
24 July		2.320						
26 July				300				
28 July		2.350						
31 July				400				

Task 1.2

Drag and drop the correct entries into the Journal below to record the following FOUR accounting transactions:

1. Receipt of metal widgets into inventory paying by BACS.
2. Issue of metal widgets from inventory to production.
3. Receipt of metal widgets into inventory paying on credit.
4. Return of metal widgets from production to inventory.

The drag and drop choices are:

- Dr. Inventory, Cr. Trade Payables' Control
- Dr. Inventory, Cr. Production
- Dr. Inventory, Cr. Bank
- Dr. Bank, Cr. Goods inward
- Dr. Trade Payables' Control, Cr. Goods inward
- Dr. Production, Cr. Inventory

	Drag and drop choice
Transaction 1	
Transaction 2	
Transaction 3	
Transaction 4	

Task 1.3

Below is a weekly timesheet for one of Savoyard Ltd's employees, who is paid as follows:

- For a basic eight-hour shift every day from Monday to Friday – basic pay.

- For any overtime in excess of the basic eight hours, on any day from Monday to Friday – the extra hours are paid at time-and-a-half (basic pay plus an overtime premium equal to half of basic pay).

- For four contracted hours each Saturday morning – basic pay.

- For any hours in excess of four hours on Saturday – the extra hours are paid at double time (basic pay plus an overtime premium equal to basic pay).

- For any hours worked on Sunday – paid at double time (basic pay plus an overtime premium equal to basic pay).

Complete the columns headed Basic pay, Overtime premium and Total pay:

(Notes: Zero figures should be entered in cells where appropriate; Overtime pay is the premium amount paid for the extra hours worked).

Employee's weekly timesheet for week ending 7 July

Employee: F. Escoffier			Cost Centre: Kitchens		
Employee number: Ch45			Basic pay per hour: £25.00		

	Hours spent on catering	Hours worked on indirect work	Notes	Basic pay £	Overtime premium £	Total pay £
Monday	8					
Tuesday	6	4	9am-1pm customer care course			
Wednesday	8					
Thursday	8					
Friday	7	1	3pm-4pm health and safety training			
Saturday	7					
Sunday	3					
Total	47	5				

Task 1.4

Claridges Ltd's budgeted overheads for the next financial year are:

	£	£
Depreciation of plant and equipment		2,010,375
Power for production machinery		1,787,500
Rent and rates		261,250
Light and heat		57,750
Indirect labour costs:		
Maintenance	252,875	
Stores	90,125	
General Administration	600,250	
Total indirect labour cost		943,250

The following information is also available:

Department	Net book value of plant and equipment	Production machinery power usage (KwH)	Floor space (square metres)	Number of employees
Production centres:				
Metal bashing	14,000,000	5,362,500		15
Metal extrusion	6,000,000	3,575,000		10
Support cost centres:				
Maintenance			35,000	5
Stores			21,000	2
General Administration			14,000	7
Total	20,000,000	8,937,500	70,000	39

Overheads are allocated or apportioned on the most appropriate basis. The total overheads of the support cost centres are then reapportioned to the two production centres using the direct method.

- 76% of the Maintenance cost centre's time is spent maintaining production machinery in the Metal bashing production centre, and the remainder in the Metal extrusion production centre.

- The Stores cost centre makes 60% of its issues to the Metal bashing production centre, and 40% to the Metal extrusion production centre.

- General Administration supports the two production centres equally.

- There is no reciprocal servicing between the three support cost centres.

Complete the table, showing the apportionment and reapportionment of overheads to the two production centres:

	Basis of apportionment	Metal bashing £	Metal extrusion £	Maintenance £	Stores £	General Admin £	Totals £
Depreciation of plant and equipment	NBV of plant and equipment						
Power for production machinery	Production machinery power usage (KwH)						
Rent and rates	Floor space						
Light and heat	Floor space						
Indirect labour	Allocated						
Totals							
Reapportion Maintenance							
Reapportion Stores							
Reapportion General Admin							
Total overheads to production centres							

Task 1.5

Next quarter Claridges Ltd's budgeted overheads and activity levels are:

	Metal bashing	Metal extrusion
Budgeted overheads (£)	814,990	445,500
Budgeted direct labour hours	40,750	24,750
Budgeted machine hours	13,145	8,250

(a) **What would be the budgeted overhead absorption rate for each department, if this were set based on their both being heavily automated?**

- [ ] Metal bashing £20/hour, Metal extrusion £18/hour
- [ ] Metal bashing £20/hour, Metal extrusion £54/hour
- [ ] Metal bashing £62/hour, Metal extrusion £18/hour
- [ ] Metal bashing £62/hour, Metal extrusion £54/hour

....

(b) **What would be the budgeted overhead absorption rate for each department, if this were set based on their both being labour intensive?**

- [ ] Metal bashing £20/hour, Metal extrusion £18/hour
- [ ] Metal bashing £20/hour, Metal extrusion £54/hour
- [ ] Metal bashing £62/hour, Metal extrusion £18/hour
- [ ] Metal bashing £62/hour, Metal extrusion £54/hour

Additional data

At the end of the quarter actual overheads incurred were found to be:

	Metal bashing	Metal extrusion
Actual overheads (£)	789,765	495,250

....

(c) **Assuming that exactly the same amount of overheads was absorbed as budgeted, what were the budgeted under- or over-absorptions in the quarter?**

- [ ] Metal bashing over-absorbed £25,225, Metal extrusion over-absorbed £49,750
- [ ] Metal bashing over-absorbed £25,225, Metal extrusion under-absorbed £49,750
- [ ] Metal bashing under-absorbed £25,225, Metal extrusion under-absorbed £49,750
- [ ] Metal bashing under-absorbed £25,225, Metal extrusion over-absorbed £49,750

....

Task 2.1

Claridges Ltd has prepared a forecast for the next quarter for one of its small Metal components, the zigger. This component is produced in batches and the forecast is based on selling and producing 3,000 batches.

One of the customers of Claridges Ltd has indicated that it may be significantly increasing its order level for the zigger for the next quarter, and it appears that activity levels of 5,000 batches and 7,000 batches are feasible.

The semi-variable costs should be calculated using the high-low method. If 7,500 batches are sold the total semi-variable cost will be £18,450, and there is a constant unit variable cost up to this volume.

Complete the table below and calculate the estimated profit per batch of the zigger at the different activity levels:

Batches produced and sold	3,000	5,000	7,000
	£	£	£
Sales revenue	90,000		
Variable costs:			
• Direct materials	13,500		
• Direct labour	31,500		
• Overheads	18,000		
Semi-variable costs:	9,450		
• Variable element			
• Fixed element			
Total cost	72,450		
Total profit	17,550		
Profit per batch (to 2 decimal places)	5.85		

Task 2.2

Claridges Ltd manufactures the alphapop, which has a selling price of £20 per unit, and a total variable cost of £12 per unit. Claridges Ltd estimates that the fixed costs per quarter associated with this product are £46,000.

(a) **Calculate the budgeted breakeven, in units, for the alphapop.**

	units

(b) **Calculate the budgeted breakeven, in £s, for the alphapop.**

£	

(c) **Complete the table below to show the budgeted margin of safety in units and the margin of safety percentage if Claridges Ltd sells 6,000 units or 7,000 units of the alphapop:**

Units of alphapop sold	6,000	7,000
	£	£
Margin of safety (units)		
Margin of safety percentage		

(d) **If Claridges Ltd wishes to make a profit of £20,000, how many units of the alphapop must it sell?**

	units

(e) **If Claridges Ltd increases the selling price of the alphapop by £5 what will be the impact on the breakeven point and the margin of safety, assuming no change in the number of units sold?**

☐	The breakeven point will decrease and the margin of safety will increase.
☐	The breakeven point will stay the same but the margin of safety will decrease.
☐	The breakeven point will decrease and the margin of safety will stay the same.
☐	The breakeven point will increase and the margin of safety will decrease.

Task 2.3

The Metal extrusion department of Claridges Ltd uses process costing for some of its products.

The process account for July for one particular process has been partly completed but the following information is also relevant:

Two employees worked on this process during July. Each employee worked 35 hours per week for 4 weeks and was paid £12.50 per hour.

Overheads are absorbed on the basis of £18 per labour hour.

Claridges Ltd expects a normal loss of 5% during this process, which it then sells for scrap at 50p per kg.

(a) Complete the process account below for July:

Description	Kgs	Unit cost £	Total cost £	Description	Kgs	Unit cost £	Total cost £
Material DD1	1,500	2.10		Normal loss		0.50	
Material DD2	1,000	1.70		Output			
Material DD3	1,000	0.65					
Labour							
Overheads							

(b) Identify the correct entry for an abnormal loss at the period end:

	Debit	Credit
Abnormal loss account		
Income statement		

Task 2.4

Claridges Ltd has the following original budget and actual performance for the BEPPO for the year ending 31 July:

	Budget	Actual
Volume sold	250,000	360,000
	£'000	£'000
Sales revenue	5,000	9,000
Less costs:		
Direct materials	875	1,325
Direct labour	1,000	1,200
Overheads	2,450	3,070
Operating profit	675	3,405

Both direct materials and direct labour are variable costs, but the overheads are fixed.

Complete the table below to show a flexed budget and the resulting variances against this budget for the year. Show the actual variance amount for sales, each cost, and operating profit, in the column headed 'Variance' and indicate whether this is Favourable or Adverse by entering F or A in the final column. If neither F nor A enter 0.

	Flexed Budget	Actual	Variance	Favourable F or Adverse A
Volume sold		360,000		
	£'000	£'000	£'000	
Sales revenue		9,000		
Less costs:				
Direct materials		1,325		
Direct labour		1,200		
Overheads		3,070		
Operating profit		3,405		

Task 2.5

One of the extrusion machines in the Metal extrusion department is nearing the end of its useful life and Claridges Ltd is considering purchasing a replacement machine.

Estimates have been made for the initial capital cost, sales income and operating costs of the replacement machine, which is expected to have a useful life of three years:

	Year 0 £'000	Year 1 £'000	Year 2 £'000	Year 3 £'000
Capital expenditure	2,250			
Other cash flows:				
Sales income		1,050	1,400	2,000
Operating costs		300	375	475

The company appraises capital investment projects using a 15% cost of capital.

(a) **Complete the table below and calculate the net present value of the proposed replacement machine (to the nearest £'000):**

	Year 0 £'000	Year 1 £'000	Year 2 £'000	Year 3 £'000
Capital expenditure				
Sales income				
Operating costs				
Net cash flows				
PV factors	1.0000	0.8696	0.7561	0.6575
Discounted cash flows				
Net present value				

The net present value is [   ] ▾ .

Picklist

Positive
Negative

(b) **Calculate the payback period of the proposed replacement machine to the nearest whole month.**

The payback period is [   ] year(s) and [   ] month(s).

....

BPP PRACTICE ASSESSMENT 1
COSTS AND REVENUES

ANSWERS

Costs and Revenues BPP practice assessment 1

Answer 1.1

(a)   The EOQ is 791 kgs = $\sqrt{\dfrac{\{2 \times 156{,}250 \times 5\}}{2.50}}$

(b) and (c) Inventory record card

Date	Receipts			Issues			Balance	
	Quantity kgs.	Cost per kg. (£)	Total cost (£)	Quantity kgs.	Cost per kg. (£)	Total cost (£)	Quantity Kgs.	Total cost (£)
Balance as at 22 July							120	276
24 July	791	2.320	1,835				911	2,111
26 July				300	2.317	695	611	1,416
28 July	791	2.350	1,859				1,402	3,275
31 July				400	2.336	934	1,002	2,341

Answer 1.2

	Drag and drop choice
Transaction 1	Dr. Inventory, Cr. Bank
Transaction 2	Dr. Production, Cr. Inventory
Transaction 3	Dr. Inventory, Cr. Trade payables' Control
Transaction 4	Dr. Inventory, Cr. Production

Answer 1.3

Employee's weekly timesheet for week ending 7 July

Employee: F. Escoffier				Cost Centre: Kitchens		
Employee number: Ch45				Basic pay per hour: £25.00		
	Hours spent on catering	Hours worked on indirect work	Notes	Basic pay £	Overtime premium £	Total pay £
Monday	8			200	0	200
Tuesday	6	4	9am-1pm customer care course	250	25	275
Wednesday	8			200	0	200
Thursday	8			200	0	200
Friday	7	1	3pm-4pm health and safety training	200	0	200
Saturday	7			175	75	250
Sunday	3			75	75	150
Total	**47**	**5**		1,300	175	1,475

Answer 1.4

	Basis of apportionment	Metal bashing £	Metal extrusion £	Maintenance £	Stores £	General Admin £	Totals £
Depreciation of plant and equipment	NBV of plant and equipment	1,407,262	603,113				2,010,375
Power for production machinery	Production machinery power usage (KwH)	1,072,500	715,000				1,787,500
Rent and rates	Floor space			130,625	78,375	52,250	261,250
Light and heat	Floor space			28,875	17,325	11,550	57,750
Indirect labour	Allocated			252,875	90,125	600,250	943,250
Totals		2,479,762	1,318,113	412,375	185,825	664,050	5,060,125
Reapportion Maintenance		313,405	98,970	(412,375)			
Reapportion Stores		111,495	74,330		(185,825)		
Reapportion General Admin		332,025	332,025			(664,050)	
Total overheads to production centres		3,236,687	1,823,438				5,060,125

Answer 1.5

(a) The correct answer is Metal bashing £62/hour, Metal extrusion £54/hour
(b) The correct answer is Metal bashing £20/hour, Metal extrusion £18/hour
(c) The correct answer is Metal bashing over-absorbed £25,225, Metal extrusion under-absorbed £49,750

Answer 2.1

Batches produced and sold	3,000	5,000	7,000
	£	£	£
Sales revenue	90,000	150,000	210,000
Variable costs:			
• Direct materials	13,500	22,500	31,500
• Direct labour	31,500	52,500	73,500
• Overheads	18,000	30,000	42,000
Semi-variable costs:	9,450		
• Variable element		10,000	14,000
• Fixed element		3,450	3,450
Total cost	72,450	118,450	164,450
Total profit	17,550	31,550	45,550
Profit per batch (to 2 decimal places)	5.85	6.31	6.51

Answer 2.2

(a) | 5,750 units |

(b) | £115,000 |

(c)

Units of alphapop sold	6,000	7,000
	£	£
Margin of safety (units)	250	1,250
Margin of safety percentage	4%	18%

(d) | 8,250 units |

(e) The correct answer is The breakeven point will decrease and the margin of safety will increase.

Answer 2.3

(a)

Description	Kgs	Unit cost £	Total cost £	Description	Kgs	Unit cost £	Total cost £
Material DD1	1,500	2.10	3,150	Normal loss	175	0.50	88
Material DD2	1,000	1.70	1,700	Output	3,325	4.20	13,952
Material DD3	1,000	0.65	650				
Labour			3,500				
Overheads			5,040				
	3,500		14,040		3,500		14,040

(b)

	Debit	Credit
Abnormal loss account		✓
Income statement	✓	

Answer 2.4

	Flexed Budget	Actual	Variance	Favourable F or Adverse A
Volume sold	360,000	360,000		
	£'000	£'000	£'000	
Sales revenue	7,200	9,000	1,800	F
Less costs:				
Direct materials	1,260	1,325	65	A
Direct labour	1,440	1,200	240	F
Overheads	2,450	3,070	620	A
Operating profit	1,430	3,405	1,975	F

Answer 2.5

(a)

	Year 0 £'000	Year 1 £'000	Year 2 £'000	Year 3 £'000
Capital expenditure	(2,250)			
Sales income		1,050	1,400	2,000
Operating costs		(300)	(375)	(475)
Net cash flows	(2,250)	750	1,025	1,525
PV factors	1.0000	0.8696	0.7561	0.6575
Discounted cash flows	(2,250)	652	775	1,003
Net present value	180			

The net present value is **positive**.

(b) The payback period is **2** years and **4** months.

BPP PRACTICE ASSESSMENT 2
COSTS AND REVENUES

Time allowed: 2½ hours

Costs and Revenues BPP practice assessment 2

Section 1

Task 1.1

The following information is available for telephone cable held by Beppo Ltd:

- Annual demand 78,125 kilograms
- Annual holding cost per kilogram £1.25
- Fixed ordering cost £2.50

(a) **Calculate the Economic Order Quantity (EOQ) for telephone cable.**

The inventory record shown below for TELEPHONE CABLE for the month of May has only been fully completed for the first three weeks of the month.

(b) **Complete the entries in the inventory record for the two receipts on 24 and 28 May that were ordered using the EOQ method.**

(c) **Complete ALL entries in the inventory record for the two issues in the month and for the closing balance at the end of May, using the FIFO method of issuing inventory.**

   (Show the costs per kilogram (kg) in £s to 3 decimal places; and the total costs in whole £s).

Inventory record for TELEPHONE CABLE

Date	Receipts			Issues			Balance	
	Quantity kgs	Cost per kg (£)	Total cost (£)	Quantity kgs	Cost per kg (£)	Total cost (£)	Quantity kgs	Total cost (£)
Balance as at 22 May							250	625
24 May		2.30						
26 May				275				
28 May		2.50						
31 May				350				

Task 1.2

Drag and drop the correct entries into the Journal below to record the following FOUR accounting transactions:

1. Issue of glass plugs from inventory to production
2. Receipt of glass plugs into inventory, paying on credit
3. Return of glass plugs from production to inventory
4. Receipt of glass plugs into inventory, paying immediately by BACS

The drag and drop choices are:

*   Dr. Payables, Cr. Work in Progress
*   Dr. Trade Payables' Control, Cr. Work in Progress
*   Dr. Inventory, Cr. Bank
*   Dr. Inventory, Cr. Trade Payables' Control
*   Dr. Inventory, Cr. Production
*   Dr. Production, Cr. Inventory

	Drag and drop choice
Transaction 1	
Transaction 2	
Transaction 3	
Transaction 4	

Task 1.3

Below is a weekly timesheet for one of Beppo Ltd's employees, who is paid as follows:

*   For a basic seven-hour shift every day from Monday to Friday – basic pay.

*   For any overtime in excess of the basic seven hours, on any day from Monday to Friday – the extra hours are paid at time-and-a-half (basic pay plus an overtime premium equal to half of basic pay).

*   For two contracted hours each Saturday morning – basic pay.

*   For any hours in excess of two hours on Saturday – the extra hours are paid at double time (basic pay plus an overtime premium equal to basic pay).

*   For any hours worked on Sunday – paid at double time (basic pay plus an overtime premium equal to basic pay).

Complete the columns headed Basic pay, Overtime premium and Total pay:

(Notes: Zero figures should be entered in cells where appropriate; Overtime pay is the premium amount paid for the extra hours worked).

Employee's weekly timesheet for week ending 7 May

Employee: G. Marx			Cost Centre: Warehouse			
Employee number: Wh45			Basic pay per hour: £15.00			
	Hours spent on direct work	Hours worked on indirect work	Notes	Basic pay £	Overtime premium £	Total pay £
Monday	7					
Tuesday	4	3	9am-1pm customer care course			
Wednesday	7					
Thursday	8					
Friday	6	1	3pm-4pm health and safety training			
Saturday	5					
Sunday	3					
Total	40	4				

Task 1.4

Beppo Ltd's budgeted overheads for the next financial year are:

	£	£
Depreciation of plant and equipment		1,005,188
Power for production machinery		893,750
Rent and rates		130,625
Light and heat		28,875
Indirect labour costs:		
Maintenance	126,438	
Stores	45,063	
General Administration	300,125	
Total indirect labour cost		471,626

The following information is also available:

Department	Net book value of plant and equipment	Production machinery power usage (KwH)	Floor space (square metres)	Number of employees
Production centres:				
Wire plaiting	7,000,000	2,681,250		12
Wire extrusion	3,000,000	1,787,500		10
Support cost centres:				
Maintenance			17,500	4
Stores			10,500	2
General Administration			7,000	3
Total	10,000,000	4,468,750	35,000	31

Overheads are allocated or apportioned on the most appropriate basis. The total overheads of the support cost centres are then reapportioned to the two production centres using the direct method.

- 55% of the Maintenance cost centre's time is spent maintaining production machinery in the Wire plaiting production centre, and the remainder in the Wire extrusion production centre.

- The Stores cost centre makes 70% of its issues to the Wire plaiting production centre, and 30% to the Wire extrusion production centre.

- General Administration supports the two production centres equally.

- There is no reciprocal servicing between the three support cost centres.

Complete the table showing the apportionment and reapportionment of overheads to the two production centres:

	Basis of apportionment	Wire plaiting £	Wire extrusion £	Maintenance £	Stores £	General Admin £	Totals £
Depreciation of plant and equipment	NBV of plant and equipment						
Power for production machinery	Production machinery power usage (KwH)						
Rent and rates	Floor space						
Light and heat	Floor space						
Indirect labour	Allocated						
Totals							
Reapportion Maintenance							
Reapportion Stores							
Reapportion General Admin							
Total overheads to production centres							

Task 1.5

Next quarter Beppo Ltd's budgeted overheads and activity levels are:

	Wire plaiting	Wire extrusion
Budgeted overheads (£)	407,495	222,750
Budgeted direct labour hours	25,750	24,750
Budgeted machine hours	11,145	8,500

(a) **What would be the budgeted overhead absorption rate for each department, if this were set based on their both being heavily automated?**

☐ Wire plaiting £16/hour, Wire extrusion £9/hour

☐ Wire plaiting £16/hour, Wire extrusion £26/hour

☐ Wire plaiting £37/hour, Wire extrusion £9/hour

☐ Wire plaiting £37/hour, Wire extrusion £26/hour

(b) **What would be the budgeted overhead absorption rate for each department, if this were set based on their both being labour intensive?**

☐ Wire plaiting £16/hour, Wire extrusion £9/hour

☐ Wire plaiting £16/hour, Wire extrusion £26/hour

☐ Wire plaiting £37/hour, Wire extrusion £9/hour

☐ Wire plaiting £37/hour, Wire extrusion £26/hour

Additional data

At the end of the quarter actual overheads incurred were found to be:

	Wire plaiting	Wire extrusion
Actual overheads (£)	425,350	247,625

(c) **Assuming that exactly the same amount of overheads was absorbed as budgeted, what were the budgeted under- or over-absorptions in the quarter?**

☐ Wire plaiting over-absorbed £17,855, Wire extrusion over-absorbed £24,875

☐ Wire plaiting over-absorbed £17,855, Wire extrusion under-absorbed £24,875

☐ Wire plaiting under-absorbed £17,855, Wire extrusion under-absorbed £24,875

☐ Wire plaiting under-absorbed £17,855, Wire extrusion over-absorbed £24,875

Task 2.1

Beppo Ltd has prepared a forecast for the next quarter for one of its small Wire components, the lagger. This component is produced in batches and the forecast is based on selling and producing 2,500 batches.

One of the customers of Beppo Ltd has indicated that it may be significantly increasing its order level for the lagger for the next quarter, and it appears that activity levels of 5,000 batches and 8,000 batches are feasible.

The semi-variable costs should be calculated using the high-low method. If 9,000 batches are sold the total semi-variable cost will be £18,450, and there is a constant unit variable cost up to this volume.

Complete the table below and calculate the estimated profit per batch of the lagger at the different activity levels:

Batches produced and sold	2,500	5,000	8,000
	£	£	£
Sales revenue	75,000		
Variable costs:			
• Direct materials	12,500		
• Direct labour	27,500		
• Overheads	15,000		
Semi-variable costs:	5,450		
• Variable element			
• Fixed element			
Total cost	60,450		
Total profit	14,550		
Profit per batch (to 2 decimal places)	5.82		

Task 2.2

Beppo Ltd manufactures the beepop, which has a selling price of £15 per unit, and a total variable cost of £6 per unit. Beppo Ltd estimates that the fixed costs per quarter associated with this product are £13,000.

(a) **Calculate the budgeted breakeven, in units, for the beepop.**

units

(b) **Calculate the budgeted breakeven, in £s, for the beepop.**

£

(c) **Complete the table below to show the budgeted margin of safety in units and the margin of safety percentage if Beppo Ltd sells 2,000 units or 2,500 units of the beepop:**

Units of beepop sold	2,000	2,500
	£	£
Margin of safety (units)		
Margin of safety percentage		

(d) **If Beppo Ltd wishes to make a profit of £50,000, how many units of the beepop must it sell?**

units

(e) **If Beppo Ltd lowers the selling price of the beepop by £1, what will be the impact on the breakeven point and the margin of safety, assuming no change in the number of units sold?**

☐ The breakeven point will decrease and the margin of safety will increase.

☐ The breakeven point will stay the same but the margin of safety will decrease.

☐ The breakeven point will decrease and the margin of safety will stay the same.

☐ The breakeven point will increase and the margin of safety will decrease.

Task 2.3

The Wire extrusion department of Beppo Ltd uses process costing for some of its products.

The process account for May for one particular process has been partly completed but the following information is also relevant:

Three employees worked on this process during May. Each employee worked 37.5 hours per week for 4 weeks and was paid £10.50 per hour.

Overheads are absorbed on the basis of £15 per labour hour.

Beppo Ltd expects a normal loss of 5% during this process, which it then sells for scrap at 75p per kg.

(a) **Complete the process account below for May:**

Description	Kgs	Unit cost £	Total cost £	Description	Kgs	Unit cost £	Total cost £
Material DD1	1,800	1.90		Normal loss		0.75	
Material DD2	1,400	1.65		Output			
Material DD3	1,000	0.95					
Labour							
Overheads							

(b) **Identify the correct entry for each of the following for an abnormal gain at the period end:**

	Debit	Credit
Abnormal gain account		
Income statement		

Task 2.4

Beppo Ltd has the following original budget and actual performance for the DEPPO for the year ending 31 May:

	Budget	Actual
Volume sold	125,000	180,000
	£'000	£'000
Sales revenue	4,500	9,000
Less costs:		
Direct materials	625	750
Direct labour	1,000	1,200
Overheads	1,225	2,450
Operating profit	1,650	4,600

Both direct materials and direct labour are variable costs, but the overheads are fixed.

Complete the table below to show a flexed budget and the resulting variances against this budget for the year. Show the actual variance amount for sales, each cost, and operating profit, in the column headed 'Variance' and indicate whether this is Favourable or Adverse by entering F or A in the final column. If neither F nor A enter 0.

	Flexed Budget	Actual	Variance	Favourable F or Adverse A
Volume sold		180,000		
	£'000	£'000	£'000	
Sales revenue		9,000		
Less costs:				
Direct materials		750		
Direct labour		1,200		
Overheads		2,450		
Operating profit		4,600		

Task 2.5

One of the extrusion machines in the Wire extrusion department is nearing the end of its useful life and Beppo Ltd is considering purchasing a replacement machine.

Estimates have been made for the initial capital cost, sales income and operating costs of the replacement machine, which is expected to have a useful life of three years:

	Year 0 £'000	Year 1 £'000	Year 2 £'000	Year 3 £'000
Capital expenditure	750			
Other cash flows:				
Sales income		700	800	750
Operating costs		250	500	500

The company appraises capital investment projects using a 10% cost of capital.

(a) **Complete the table below and calculate the net present value of the proposed replacement machine (to the nearest £'000):**

	Year 0 £'000	Year 1 £'000	Year 2 £'000	Year 3 £'000
Capital expenditure				
Sales income				
Operating costs				
Net cash flows				
PV factors	1.0000	0.9091	0.8264	0.7513
Discounted cash flows				
Net present value				

The net present value is [   ] ▼

Picklist

Positive

Negative

(b) **Calculate the payback period of the proposed replacement machine to the nearest whole month.**

The payback period is [   ] year(s) and [   ] month(s).

BPP PRACTICE ASSESSMENT 2
COSTS AND REVENUES

ANSWERS

Costs and Revenues BPP practice assessment 2

Answer 1.1

(a) The EOQ is 559 kgs = $\sqrt{\dfrac{2 \times 78,125 \times 2.5}{1.25}}$

(b) and (c) Inventory record card

Date	Receipts Quantity kgs	Cost per kg (£)	Total cost (£)	Issues Quantity kgs	Cost per kg (£)	Total cost (£)	Balance Quantity kgs	Total cost (£)
Balance as at 22 May							250	625
24 May	559	2.30	1,286				809	1,911
26 May				275	2.50/2.30	683	534	1,228
28 May	559	2.50	1,398				1,093	2,626
31 May				350	2.30	805	743	1,821

Answer 1.2

	Drag and drop choice
Transaction 1	Dr. Production, Cr. Inventory
Transaction 2	Dr. Inventory, Cr. Trade payables' Control
Transaction 3	Dr. Inventory, Cr. Production
Transaction 4	Dr. Inventory, Cr. Bank

Answer 1.3

Employee's weekly timesheet for week ending 7 May

Employee: G. Marx			Cost Centre: Warehouse			
Employee number: Wh45			Basic pay per hour: £15.00			
	Hours spent on direct work	Hours worked on indirect work	Notes	Basic pay £	Overtime premium £	Total pay £
Monday	7			105	0	105
Tuesday	4	3	9am-1pm customer care course	105	0	105
Wednesday	7			105	0	105
Thursday	8			120	7.50	127.50
Friday	6	1	3pm-4pm health and safety training	105	0	105
Saturday	5			75	45	120
Sunday	3			45	45	90
Total	40	4		660	97.50	757.50

Answer 1.4

	Basis of apportionment	Wire plaiting £	Wire extrusion £	Maintenance £	Stores £	General Admin £	Totals £
Depreciation of plant and equipment	NBV of plant and equipment	703,632	301,556				1,005,188
Power for production machinery	Production machinery power usage (KwH)	536,250	357,500				893,750
Rent and rates	Floor space			65,312	39,188	26,125	130,625
Light and heat	Floor space			14,438	8,662	5,775	28,875
Indirect labour	Allocated			126,438	45,063	300,125	471,626
Totals		1,239,882	659,056	206,188	92,913	332,025	2,530,064
Reapportion Maintenance		113,403	92,785	(206,188)			
Reapportion Stores		65,039	27,874		(92,913)		
Reapportion General Admin		166,012	166,013			(332,025)	
Total overheads to production centres		1,584,336	945,728				2,530,064

....

Answer 1.5

(a) The correct answer is Wire plaiting £37/hour, Wire extrusion £26/hour
(b) The correct answer is Wire plaiting £16/hour, Wire extrusion £9/hour
(c) The correct answer is Wire plaiting under-absorbed £17,855, Wire extrusion under-absorbed £24,875

....

Answer 2.1

Batches produced and sold	2,500	5,000	8,000
	£	£	£
Sales revenue	75,000	150,000	240,000
Variable costs:			
• Direct materials	12,500	25,000	40,000
• Direct labour	27,500	55,000	88,000
• Overheads	15,000	30,000	48,000
Semi-variable costs:	5,450		
• Variable element		10,000	16,000
• Fixed element		450	450
Total cost	60,450	120,450	192,450
Total profit	14,550	29,550	47,550
Profit per batch (to 2 decimal places)	5.82	5.91	5.94

Answer 2.2

(a) | 1,444 units |

(b) | £21,660 |

(c)

Units of beebop sold	2,000	2,500
	£	£
Margin of safety (units)	556	1,056
Margin of safety percentage	28%	42%

(d) | 7,000 units |

(e) The correct answer is The breakeven point will increase and the margin of safety will decrease.

Answer 2.3

(a)

Description	Kgs	Unit cost £	Total cost £	Description	Kgs	Unit cost £	Total cost £
Material DD1	1,800	1.90	3,420	Normal loss	210	0.75	158
Material DD2	1,400	1.65	2,310	Output	3,990	4.51	17,997
Material DD3	1,000	0.95	950				
Labour			4,725				
Overheads			6,750				
	4,200		18,155		4,200		18,155

(b)

	Debit	Credit
Abnormal gain account	✓	
Income statement		✓

Answer 2.4

	Flexed Budget	Actual	Variance	Favourable F or Adverse A
Volume sold	180,000	180,000		
	£'000	£'000	£'000	
Sales revenue	6,480	9,000	2,520	F
Less costs:				
Direct materials	900	750	150	F
Direct labour	1,440	1,200	240	F
Overheads	1,225	2,450	1,225	A
Operating profit	1,690	4,600	2,910	F

Answer 2.5

(a)

	Year 0 £'000	Year 1 £'000	Year 2 £'000	Year 3 £'000
Capital expenditure	(750)			
Sales income		700	800	750
Operating costs		(250)	(500)	(500)
Net cash flows	(750)	450	300	250
PV factors	1.0000	0.9091	0.8264	0.7513
Discounted cash flows	(750)	409	248	188
Net present value	95			

The net present value is *positive*.

(b) The payback period is *2* years.

BPP PRACTICE ASSESSMENT 3
COSTS AND REVENUES

Time allowed: 2½ hours

Costs and Revenues BPP practice assessment 3

Section 1

Task 1.1

Livia Ltd orders in the Zippo. The following information is available for the Zippo:

- Annual demand 55,000 kilograms
- Annual holding cost per kilogram £1.25
- Fixed ordering cost £1.75

(a) Calculate the Economic Order Quantity (EOQ) for the Zippo.

The inventory record shown below for the ZIPPO for the month of June has only been fully completed for the first three weeks of the month.

(b) Complete the entries in the inventory record for the two receipts on 24 and 28 June that were ordered using the EOQ method.

(c) Complete ALL entries in the inventory record for the two issues in the month and for the closing balance at the end of June, using the LIFO method of issuing inventory.

(Show the costs per kilogram (kg) in £s to 3 decimal places; and the total costs in whole £s).

Inventory record for the ZIPPO

Date	Receipts			Issues			Balance	
	Quantity kgs	Cost per kg (£)	Total cost (£)	Quantity kgs	Cost per kg (£)	Total cost (£)	Quantity kgs	Total cost (£)
Balance as at 22 June							500	625
24 June		1.305						
26 June				400				
28 June		1.310						
30 June				200				

Task 1.2

Drag and drop the correct entries into the Journal below to record the following FOUR accounting transactions:

1. Return of fibre optic cable from production to inventory
2. Receipt of fibre optic cable into inventory, paying immediately by BACS
3. Issue of fibre optic cable from inventory to production
4. Receipt of fibre optic cable into inventory, paying on credit

The drag and drop choices are:

- Dr. Trade Payables' Control, Cr. Inventory
- Dr. Bank, Cr. Inventory
- Dr. Inventory, Cr. Trade Payables' Control
- Dr. Inventory, Cr. Bank
- Dr. Production, Cr. Inventory
- Dr. Inventory, Cr. Production

	Drag and drop choice
Transaction 1	
Transaction 2	
Transaction 3	
Transaction 4	

Task 1.3

Below is a weekly timesheet for one of Avila Ltd's employees, who is paid as follows:

- For a basic six-hour shift every day from Monday to Friday - basic pay.

- For any overtime in excess of the basic six hours, on any day from Monday to Friday - the extra hours are paid at time-and-a-quarter (basic pay plus an overtime premium equal to quarter of basic pay).

- For two contracted hours each Saturday morning - basic pay.

- For any hours in excess of two hours on Saturday - the extra hours are paid at time-and-a-half (basic pay plus an overtime premium equal to a half of basic pay).

- For any hours worked on Sunday - paid at double time (basic pay plus an overtime premium equal to basic pay).

Complete the columns headed Basic pay, Overtime premium and Total pay:

(Notes: Zero figures should be entered in cells where appropriate; Overtime pay is the premium amount paid for the extra hours worked).

Employee's weekly timesheet for week ending 7 June

Employee: C. Cross			Cost Centre: Plating			
Employee number: P53			Basic pay per hour: £13.00			
	Hours spent on production	Hours worked on indirect work	Notes	Basic pay £	Overtime premium £	Total pay £
Monday	8					
Tuesday	2	4	9am-1pm customer care course			
Wednesday	6	2	12am-2pm paperwork			
Thursday	6					
Friday	5	1	1pm-2pm fire safety training			
Saturday	6					
Sunday	3					
Total	36	7				

Task 1.4

Tagus Ltd's budgeted overheads for the next financial year are:

	£	£
Depreciation of plant and equipment		750,500
Power for production machinery		1,875,000
Rent and rates		120,500
Light and heat		32,500
Indirect labour costs:		
Maintenance	115,000	
Stores	37,850	
General Administration	225,000	
Total indirect labour cost		377,850

The following information is also available:

Department	Net book value of plant and equipment	Production machinery power usage (KwH)	Floor space (square metres)	Number of employees
Production centres:				
Glass moulding	1,250,000	225,000		7
Glass extrusion	1,750,000	185,000		5
Support cost centres:				
Maintenance			10,000	4
Stores			12,000	5
General Administration			8,000	2
Total	3,000,000	410,000	30,000	23

Overheads are allocated or apportioned on the most appropriate basis. The total overheads of the support cost centres are then reapportioned to the two production centres using the direct method.

- 45% of the Maintenance cost centre's time is spent maintaining production machinery in the Glass moulding production centre, and the remainder in the Glass extrusion production centre.

- The Stores cost centre makes 35% of its issues to the Glass moulding production centre, and 65% to the Glass extrusion production centre.

- General Administration supports the two production centres equally.

- There is no reciprocal servicing between the three support cost centres.

Complete the table showing the apportionment and reapportionment of overheads to the two production centres:

	Basis of apportionment	Glass moulding £	Glass extrusion £	Maintenance £	Stores £	General Admin £	Totals £
Depreciation of plant and equipment	NBV of plant and equipment						
Power for production machinery	Production machinery power usage (KwH)						
Rent and rates	Floor space						
Light and heat	Floor space						
Indirect labour	Allocated						
Totals							
Reapportion Maintenance							
Reapportion Stores							
Reapportion General Admin							
Total overheads to production centres							

Task 1.5

Next quarter Tagus Ltd's budgeted overheads and activity levels are:

	Glass moulding	Glass extrusion
Budgeted overheads (£)	280,650	300,115
Budgeted direct labour hours	15,550	18,450
Budgeted machine hours	4,350	6,745

(a) **What would be the budgeted overhead absorption rate for each department, if this were set based on their both being heavily automated?**

☐ Glass moulding £65/hour, Glass extrusion £16/hour

☐ Glass moulding £18/hour, Glass extrusion £44/hour

☐ Glass moulding £65/hour, Glass extrusion £44/hour

☐ Glass moulding £18/hour, Glass extrusion £16/hour

(b) **What would be the budgeted overhead absorption rate for each department, if this were set based on their both being labour intensive?**

☐ Glass moulding £65/hour, Glass extrusion £16/hour

☐ Glass moulding £18/hour, Glass extrusion £44/hour

☐ Glass moulding £65/hour, Glass extrusion £44/hour

☐ Glass moulding £18/hour, Glass extrusion £16/hour

Additional data

At the end of the quarter actual overheads incurred were found to be:

	Glass moulding	Glass extrusion
Actual overheads (£)	315,906	285,550

(c) **Assuming that exactly the same amount of overheads was absorbed as budgeted, what were the budgeted under- or over-absorptions in the quarter?**

☐ Glass moulding over-absorbed £35,256, Glass extrusion over-absorbed £14,565

☐ Glass moulding over-absorbed £35,256, Glass extrusion under-absorbed £14,565

☐ Glass moulding under-absorbed £35,256, Glass extrusion under-absorbed £14,565

☐ Glass moulding under-absorbed £35,256, Glass extrusion over-absorbed £14,565

Task 2.1

Lisboa Ltd has prepared a forecast for the next quarter for one of its small plastic components, ZEST. This component is produced in batches and the forecast is based on selling and producing 2,400 batches.

One of the customers of Lisboa Ltd has indicated that it may be significantly increasing its order level for component ZEST for the next quarter and it appears that activity levels of 3,500 batches and 4,000 batches are feasible.

The semi-variable costs should be calculated using the high-low method. If 6,000 batches are sold the total semi-variable cost will be £14,754, and there is a constant unit variable cost up to this volume.

Complete the table below and calculate the estimated profit per batch of ZEST at the different activity levels:

Batches produced and sold	2,400	3,500	4,000
	£	£	£
Sales revenue	45,500		
Variable costs:			
• Direct materials	11,250		
• Direct labour	10,850		
• Overheads	6,825		
Semi-variable costs:	8,400		
• Variable element			
• Fixed element			
Total cost	37,325		
Total profit	8,175		
Profit per batch (to 2 decimal places)	3.41		

Task 2.2

Product TEST has a selling price of £32 per unit with a total variable cost of £24 per unit. Avignon Ltd estimates that the fixed costs per quarter associated with this product are £43,000.

(a) Calculate the budgeted breakeven, in units, for product TEST.

units

(b) Calculate the budgeted breakeven, in £s, for product TEST.

£

(c) Complete the table below to show the budgeted margin of safety in units and the margin of safety percentage if Avignon Ltd sells 5,500 units or 7,000 units of product TEST:

Units of TEST sold	5,500	7,000
	£	£
Margin of safety (units)		
Margin of safety percentage		

(d) If Avignon Ltd wishes to make a profit of £35,000, how many units of TEST must it sell?

units

(e) If Avignon Ltd decreases the selling price of TEST by 10p what will be the impact on the breakeven point and the margin of safety, assuming no change in the number of units sold?

	The breakeven point will decrease and the margin of safety will increase.
	The breakeven point will stay the same but the margin of safety will decrease.
	The breakeven point will increase and the margin of safety will decrease.
	The breakeven point will increase and the margin of safety stay the same.

Task 2.3

The Glass moulding department of Seville Ltd uses process costing for some of its products.

The process account for June for one particular process has been partly completed but the following information is also relevant:

Two employees worked on this process during June. Each employee worked 35 hours per week for 4 weeks and was paid £14 per hour.

Overheads are absorbed on the basis of £17 per labour hour.

Seville Ltd expects a normal loss of 7.5% during this process, which it then sells for scrap at 50p per kg.

(a) Complete the process account below for June:

Description	Kgs	Unit cost £	Total cost £	Description	Kgs	Unit cost £	Total cost £
Material G4	700	1.30		Normal loss		0.50	
Material G3	500	1.40		Output			
Material G9	500	1.10					
Labour							
Overheads							

(b) Identify the correct journal entries for an abnormal loss:

	Debit	Credit
Process account		
Abnormal loss account		

Task 2.4

Bilbao Ltd has the following original budget and actual performance for product SCOOT for the year ending 30 June:

	Budget	Actual
Volume sold	50,000	44,000
	£'000	£'000
Sales revenue	1,750	1,496
Less costs:		
Direct materials	150	130
Direct labour	200	280
Overheads	950	928
Operating profit	450	158

Both direct materials and direct labour are variable costs, but the overheads are fixed.

Complete the table below to show a flexed budget and the resulting variances against this budget for the year. Show the actual variance amount for sales, each cost, and operating profit, in the column headed 'Variance' and indicate whether this is Favourable or Adverse by entering F or A in the final column. If neither F nor A enter 0.

	Flexed Budget	Actual	Variance	Favourable F or Adverse A
Volume sold		44,000		
	£'000	£'000	£'000	
Sales revenue		1,496		
Less costs:				
Direct materials		130		
Direct labour		280		
Overheads		928		
Operating profit		158		

Task 2.5

One of the moulding machines in the Glass extrusion department is nearing the end of its useful life and Bilbao Ltd is considering purchasing a replacement machine.

Estimates have been made for the initial capital cost, sales income and operating costs of the replacement machine, which is expected to have a useful life of three years:

	Year 0 £'000	Year 1 £'000	Year 2 £'000	Year 3 £'000
Capital expenditure	900			
Other cash flows:				
Sales income		540	660	780
Operating costs		300	310	320

The company appraises capital investment projects using a 12% cost of capital.

(a) **Complete the table below and calculate the net present value of the proposed replacement machine (to the nearest £'000):**

	Year 0 £'000	Year 1 £'000	Year 2 £'000	Year 3 £'000
Capital expenditure				
Sales income				
Operating costs				
Net cash flows				
PV factors	1.0000	0.8929	0.7972	0.7118
Discounted cash flows				
Net present value				

The net present value is [＿＿＿＿＿＿] ▼

Picklist

Positive
Negative

(b) Calculate the payback period of the proposed replacement machine to the nearest whole month.

The payback period is [   ] year(s) and [   ] month(s).

BPP PRACTICE ASSESSMENT 3
COSTS AND REVENUES

ANSWERS

Costs and Revenues BPP practice assessment 3

Answer 1.1

(a) The EOQ is 392 kgs = $\sqrt{\dfrac{\{2 \times 55,000 \times 1.75\}}{1.25}}$

(b) and (c) Inventory record card

Date	Receipts Quantity kgs	Receipts Cost per kg (£)	Receipts Total cost (£)	Issues Quantity kgs	Issues Cost per kg (£)	Issues Total cost (£)	Balance Quantity kgs	Balance Total cost (£)
Balance as at 22 June							500	625
24 June	392	1.305	512				892	1,137
26 June				400	1.305/1.25	522	492	615
28 June	392	1.310	514				884	1,129
30 June				200	1.310	262	684	867

Answer 1.2

	Drag and drop choice
Transaction 1	Dr. Inventory, Cr. Production
Transaction 2	Dr. Inventory, Cr. Bank
Transaction 3	Dr. Production, Cr. Inventory
Transaction 4	Dr. Inventory, Cr. Trade payables' Control

Answer 1.3

Employee's weekly timesheet for week ending 7 June

Employee: C. Cross			Cost Centre: Plating		
Employee number: P53			Basic pay per hour: £13.00		
	Hours spent on production	Hours worked on indirect work	Notes	Basic pay £	Overtime premium £	Total pay £
Monday	8			104.00	6.50	110.50
Tuesday	2	4	9am-1pm customer care course	78.00	0	78.00
Wednesday	6	2	12am-2pm paperwork	104.00	6.50	110.50
Thursday	6			78.00	0	78.00
Friday	5	1	1pm-2pm fire safety training	78.00	0	78.00
Saturday	6			78.00	26.00	104.00
Sunday	3			39.00	39.00	78.00
Total	**36**	**7**		559.00	78.00	637.00

Answer 1.4

	Basis of apportionment	Glass moulding £	Glass extrusion £	Maintenance £	Stores £	General Admin £	Totals £
Depreciation of plant and equipment	NBV of plant and equipment	312,708	437,792				750,500
Power for production machinery	Production machinery power usage (KwH)	1,028,963	846,037				1,875,000
Rent and rates	Floor space			40,167	48,200	32,133	120,500
Light and heat	Floor space			10,833	13,000	8,667	32,500
Indirect labour	Allocated			115,000	37,850	225,000	377,850
Totals		1,341,671	1,283,829	166,000	99,050	265,800	3,156,350
Reapportion Maintenance		74,700	91,300	(166,000)			
Reapportion Stores		34,668	64,382		(99,050)		
Reapportion General Admin		132,900	132,900			(265,800)	
Total overheads to production centres		1,583,939	1,572,411				3,156,350

Answer 1.5

(a) The correct answer is Glass moulding £65/hour, Glass extrusion £44/hour
(b) The correct answer is Glass moulding £18/hour, Glass extrusion £16/hour
(c) The correct answer is Glass moulding under-absorbed £35,256, Glass extrusion over-absorbed £14,565

Answer 2.1

Batches produced and sold	2,400	3,500	4,000
	£	£	£
Sales revenue	45,500	65,354	75,833
Variable costs:			
• Direct materials	11,250	16,406	18,750
• Direct labour	10,850	15,823	18,083
• Overheads	6,825	9,953	11,375
Semi-variable costs:	8,400		
• Variable element		6,178	7,060
• Fixed element		4,164	4,164
Total cost	37,325	52,524	59,432
Total profit	8,175	12,830	16,401
Profit per batch (to 2 decimal places)	3.41	3.67	4.10

Answer 2.2

(a) 5,375 units

(b) £172,000

(c)

Units of TEST sold	5,500	7,000
	£	£
Margin of safety (units)	125	1,625
Margin of safety percentage	2%	23%

(d) 9,750 units

(e) The correct answer is The breakeven point will increase and the margin of safety will decrease.

Answer 2.3

(a)

Description	Kgs	Unit cost £	Total cost £	Description	Kgs	Unit cost £	Total cost £
Material G4	700	1.30	910	Normal loss	128	0.50	64
Material G3	500	1.40	700	Output	1,572	6.85	10,776
Material G9	500	1.10	550				
Labour			3,920				
Overheads			4,760				
	1,700		10,840		1,700		10,840

(b)

	Debit	Credit
Process account		✓
Abnormal loss account	✓	

Answer 2.4

	Flexed Budget	Actual	Variance	Favourable F or Adverse A
Volume sold	44,000	44,000		
	£'000	£'000	£'000	
Sales revenue	1,540	1,496	44	A
Less costs:				
Direct materials	132	130	2	F
Direct labour	176	280	104	A
Overheads	950	928	22	F
Operating profit	304	158	146	A

Answer 2.5

(a)

	Year 0 £'000	Year 1 £'000	Year 2 £'000	Year 3 £'000
Capital expenditure	(900)			
Sales income		540	660	780
Operating costs		(300)	(310)	(320)
Net cash flows	(900)	240	350	460
PV factors	1.0000	0.8929	0.7972	0.7118
Discounted cash flows	(900)	214	279	327
Net present value	(80)			

The net present value is *negative*.

(b) The payback period is *2* years and *8* months.

BPP PRACTICE ASSESSMENT 4
COSTS AND REVENUES

Time allowed: 2½ hours

Costs and Revenues BPP practice assessment 4

Section 1

Task 1.1

(a) **Choose the correct words from the drop down menu to complete the paragraph.**

If costs are increasing, FIFO/LIFO will give a higher profit than FIFO/LIFO as issues, which form cost of sales, are at the earlier, LOWER/HIGHER prices.

The weighted average method GIVES A HIGHER PROFIT THAN LIFO AND FIFO/GIVES A LOWER PROFIT THAN FIFO AND LIFO/FALLS SOMEWHERE IN BETWEEN THE PROFITS GIVEN BY FIFO AND LIFO.

In the long-term, over the life of the business, any such differences will DISAPPEAR/GIVE THE BUSINESS AN ADVANTAGE/GIVE THE BUSINESS A DISADVANTAGE

(b)

The following data relate to inventory item HMF2.

Average usage	200 units per day
Lead time	16 – 20 days
Reorder level	5,700

What is the approximate number of HMF2 parts carried as buffer inventory?

units

(c) **Which of the following is the correct formula for the economic order quantity?**

☐ $EOQ = \sqrt{\dfrac{2cd}{h}}$

☐ $EOQ = \sqrt{\dfrac{2hd}{c}}$

☐ $EOQ = \dfrac{\sqrt{2hd}}{c}$

☐ $EOQ = \dfrac{\sqrt{2cd}}{h}$

Where
h is the cost of holding one unit in inventory for one year
d is the annual demand
c is the cost of placing an order

Task 1.2

The material stores control account for a company for March looks like this:

Material stores control account

	£		£
Balance b/d	30,000	Work in progress	100,000
Suppliers	122,500	Overhead control	30,000
Work in progress	45,000	Balance c/d	67,500
	197,500		197,500
Balance b/d	67,500		

Which of the following statements are correct?

(i) Issues of direct materials during March were £45,000

(ii) Issues of direct materials during March were £100,000

(iii) Issues of indirect materials during March were £30,000

(iv) Purchases of materials during March were £122,500

☐ (i) and (iv) only

☐ (ii) and (iv) only

☐ (ii), (iii) and (iv) only

☐ All of them

Task 1.3

(a) Complete the columns headed Direct wages and Indirect wages.

(Notes: Zero figures should be entered in cells where appropriate).

			Direct wages £	Indirect wages £
Basic 35 hours per week at £10 per hour				
Overtime of 4 hours due to machine breakdown				
	Basic 4 hrs @ £10			
	Premium 4 hrs @ £5			
Overtime of 2 hrs at the request of customer				
	Basic 2 hrs @ £10			
	Premium 2 hrs @ £5			
Total				

- -

(b) An employee is paid on a differential piecework system on the following basis.

Up to 750 units produced a week   £2.50 per unit

Units over 750 and up to 1,000   £2.88 per unit

Any units over 1,000   £3.35 per unit

In the week ending 29 June the employee produced 1,075 units. **What is his total gross pay for the week?**

£

- -

Task 1.4

A manufacturing organisation has two production departments, A and B, and two service cost centres, stores and the canteen.

The budgeted overheads for the next period are as follows:

	Total £	A £	B £	Stores £	Canteen £
Indirect wages	75,700	7,800	4,700	21,200	42,000
Rent	24,000				
Buildings insurance	2,000				
Power	6,400				
Heat and light	4,000				
Supervisor's wages – Dept A	10,000				
Machinery depreciation	3,200				
Machinery insurance	2,200				
Total					
Canteen					(49,730)
Stores					

You are also provided with the following information:

	Total	A	B	Stores	Canteen
Net book value of machinery	£300,000	£140,000	£120,000	£15,000	£25,000
Power usage (%)	100%	45%	30%	5%	20%
Number of employees	126	70	40	10	6
Supervisor's hours	40	25	15		
Floor area (sq m)	30,000	12,000	8,000	4,000	6,000
Materials requisitions	500	300	200		

The stores staff use the canteen but the canteen makes no use of the stores services.

You are required to:

(a) allocate or apportion the overheads to each of the production and service cost centres on a fair basis. (Work to the nearest whole £.)

(b) reapportion the service cost centre costs to the production cost centres using the step down method. (Work to the nearest whole £.)

Task 1.5

(a) Budgeted machine hours   17,000

Actual machine hours   21,250

Budgeted overheads   £85,000

Actual overheads   £110,500

Based on the data above:

The machine hour absorption rate is £ [　　　] **per hour.**

The overhead for the period was [　　　] **absorbed by £** [　　　]

(b) **The accounting entries at the end of a period for production overhead under-absorbed would be** (tick the correct boxes):

	Debit	Credit	No entry in this a/c
Overhead control account			
Work in progress account			
Income statement			

(c) The overhead absorption rate for product M is £8 per machine hour. Each unit of M requires 1 machine hour. Inventories of product M last period were:

	Units
Opening inventory	6,000
Closing inventory	6,750

The absorption costing profit for the period for product M will be:

[　] higher

[　] lower

than the marginal costing profit. **The difference between the two profit figures will be**

£ [　　　　　　　]

Task 2.1

CCC Ltd has prepared a forecast for the next quarter for one of its products. The products are produced in batches and the forecast is based on selling and producing 4,000 batches.

The managing director would like to expand the business and is interested to know the profits that could be made if 6,000 batches were made and sold and 9,000 batches were made and sold.

The semi-variable costs should be calculated using the high-low method. If 6,500 batches are sold the total semi-variable cost will be £24,250, and there is a constant unit variable cost up to this volume.

Complete the table below and calculate the estimated profit per batch of the product at the different activity levels:

Batches produced and sold	4,000	6,000	9,000
	£	£	£
Sales revenue	140,000		
Variable costs:			
• Direct materials	22,000		
• Direct labour	50,000		
• Overheads	28,000		
Semi-variable costs:	16,750		
Total cost	116,750		
Total profit	23,250		
Profit per batch (to 2 decimal places)	5.81		

Task 2.2

ABC Co, is a company producing and selling two types of toys: the elephant and the giraffe. The expected monthly costs and sales information for each toy is as follows.

Toy	Elephant	Giraffe
Sales and production quantity	1,250	1,750
Labour hours per month	120	100
Total sales revenue	£2,500	£3,500
Total direct materials	£200	£350
Total direct labour	£750	£875
Total variable overheads	£50	£140

The total expected monthly fixed costs relating to the production of all toys is £750.

(a) **You are required to complete the table below to show the profit volume ratio for each toy.**

Toy	Elephant £	Giraffe £
Selling price per toy		
Less: Unit variable costs		
Direct materials		
Direct labour		
Variable overheads		
Contribution per toy		
Profit volume ratio (%)		

(b) **ABC has decided stop making elephant toys. The expected monthly fixed costs remain at £750. Calculate the breakeven point to the nearest whole unit.**

[   ] units

(c) **Calculate the margin of safety.**

[   ] units

Task 2.3

A business produces three products. Production and sales details are given below:

	Product		
	J	K	L
Direct materials @ £6 per kg	£12	£30	£18
Direct labour @ £8 per hour	£16	£32	£32
Selling price	£65	£70	£60
Machine hours per unit	4	3	2
Maximum sales demand	50,000 units	62,500 units	20,000 units

During the next period the supply of materials is limited to 490,000 kgs, the labour hours available are 400,000 and the machine hours available are 430,000.

Fill in the tables below to decide whether there are any limiting resources.

(a)

	J	K	L	Total
Material requirements				
Kg needed per unit				
Maximum sales demand				
Total kg needed				
Total kg available				

Material Shortage?

Picklist

Yes
No

BPP
LEARNING MEDIA

	J	K	L	Total
Labour hour requirements				
Labour hours needed per unit				
Maximum sales demand				
Total labour hours needed				
Total labour hours available				

Labour hour shortage?

Picklist

Yes
No

	J	K	L	Total
Machine hour requirements				
Machine hours needed per unit				
Maximum sales demand				
Total machine hours needed				
Total machine hours available				

Machine hour shortage?

Picklist

Yes
No

(b) Calculate contribution per labour hour and rank the products in order to maximise contribution.

	J	K	L
Contribution per unit			
Labour hours per unit			
Contribution per labour hour			
Ranking			

(c) Prepare the production plan which will maximise contribution

Product letter	Units	Labour hours used	Cumulative labour hours used
			400,000

Task 2.4

Jumbo Ltd has the following original budget and actual performance for the year ending 31 May:

	Budget	Actual
Volume sold	300,000	410,000
	£'000	£'000
Sales revenue	9,000	14,350
Less costs:		
Direct materials	1,650	2,460
Direct labour	1,350	1,640
Overheads	3,250	4,010
Operating profit	2,750	6,240

Both direct materials and direct labour are variable costs, but the overheads are fixed.

Complete the table below to show a flexed budget and the resulting variances against this budget for the year. Show the actual variance amount for sales, each cost, and operating profit, in the column headed 'Variance' and indicate whether this is Favourable or Adverse by entering F or A in the final column. If the variance is neither F nor A, enter 0.

	Flexed Budget	Actual	Variance	Favourable F or Adverse A
Volume sold		410,000		
	£'000	£'000	£'000	
Sales revenue		14,350		
Less costs:				
Direct materials		2,460		
Direct labour		1,640		
Overheads		4,010		
Operating profit		6,240		

Task 2.5

(a) Choose the correct word from the pick list.

The internal rate of return (IRR) is the discount rate that will result in a [_____▼] net present value.

Picklist

Positive
Negative
Zero

If the IRR of a project is [_____▼] than the organisation's cost of capital then the project should be accepted.

Picklist

Higher
Lower

IRR [_____▼] take into account the time value of money.

Picklist

Does
Does not

(b) A project has the following budgeted costs and inflows.

Initial cost	(£350,000)
Inflow 1 year later	£150,000
Inflow 2 years' later	£75,000
Inflow 3 years' later	£95,000
Inflow 4 years' later	£90,000

Calculate the payback period of the proposed project to the nearest whole month.

The payback period is [_____] year(s) and [_____] month(s).

(c) A project has achieved a net present value of £6,000. What does this indicate?

[ ] The project should be rejected

[ ] The project should be accepted

[ ] The project will make £6,000 profit

[ ] The project will generate £6,000 in cash over its life

BPP PRACTICE ASSESSMENT 4
COSTS AND REVENUES

ANSWERS

Costs and Revenues BPP practice assessment 4

Answer 1.1

(a)

If costs are increasing, FIFO will give a higher profit than LIFO as issues, which form cost of sales, are at the earlier, LOWER prices.

The weighted average method FALLS SOMEWHERE IN BETWEEN THE PROFITS GIVEN BY FIFO AND LIFO.

In the long-term, over the life of the business, any such differences will DISAPPEAR

(b)

2,100

Buffer inventory = reorder level – (average usage × average lead time)

$$= 5,700 - (200 \times 18)$$

$$= 2,100$$

(c) $EOQ = \sqrt{\dfrac{2cd}{h}}$

....

Answer 1.2

(ii), (iii) and (iv) only

Statement (i) is not correct. A debit to materials with a corresponding credit to work in progress (WIP) indicates that direct materials returned from production were £45,000.

Statement (ii) is correct. Direct costs of production are 'collected' in the WIP account.

Statement (iii) is correct. Indirect costs of production or overhead are 'collected' in the overhead control account.

Statement (iv) is correct. The purchases of materials on credit are credited to the payables account and debited to the materials control account.

....

Answer 1.3

(a)

				Direct wages £	Indirect wages £
Basic 35 hours per week at £10 per hour				350	
Overtime of 4 hours due to machine breakdown					
		Basic 4 hrs @ £10		40	
		Premium 4 hrs @ £5			20
Overtime of 2 hrs at the request of customer					
		Basic 2 hrs @£10		20	
		Premium 2 hrs @ £5		10	
Total				420	20

(b)

	£
750 units @ £2.50	1,875
250 units @ £2.88	720
75 units @ £3.35	251.25
	2,846.25

Answer 1.4

	Total £	A £	B £	Stores £	Canteen £
Indirect wages	75,700	7,800	4,700	21,200	42,000
Rent	24,000	9,600	6,400	3,200	4,800
Buildings insurance	2,000	800	533	267	400
Power	6,400	2,880	1,920	320	1,280
Heat and light	4,000	1,600	1,066	534	800
Supervisor's wages	10,000	10,000	–	–	–
Machinery depreciation	3,200	1,493	1,280	160	267
Machinery insurance	2,200	1,027	880	110	183
Total	127,500	35,200	16,779	25,791	49,730
Canteen		29,009	16,577	4,144	(49,730)
				29,935	
Stores		17,961	11,974	(29,935)	
		82,170	45,330	–	–

Workings

Rent, buildings insurance and heat and light are apportioned on the basis of floor area – 12:8:4:6.

Power is apportioned using the percentages given.

Supervisor's wages are allocated directly to department A.

Machinery depreciation and insurance are apportioned on the basis of the net book value of the machinery – 140:120:15:25.

Canteen costs are apportioned according to the number of staff that use it – 70:40:10.

The stores costs are apportioned on the basis of the number of materials requisitions.

Answer 1.5

(a) The machine hour absorption rate is £ [5] per hour.

$$\text{Overhead absorption rate} = \frac{\text{Budgeted overheads}}{\text{Budgeted machine hours}}$$

$$= \frac{£85,000}{17,000}$$

$$= £5$$

The overhead for the period was [under] absorbed by £ [4,250]

$$\text{Overhead over-/(under)-absorbed} = \text{Overhead absorbed} - \text{Overhead incurred}$$

$$= (21,250 \times £5) - £110,500$$

$$= £(4,250)$$

(b)

	Debit £	Credit £	No entry in this a/c £
Overhead control account		✓	
Work in progress account			✓
Income statement	✓		

Under-absorbed overhead means that the overhead charged to production was too low and so there must be a debit to the income statement.

(c) The absorption costing profit for the period for product M will be:

[✓] higher

than the marginal costing profit. The difference between the two profit figures will be

£ [6,000]

Difference in profit = change in inventory level × fixed overhead per unit

$$= (6,000 - 6,750) \times (£8 \times 1)$$

$$= £6,000$$

The absorption costing profit will be higher because inventories have increased, and fixed overheads have been carried forward in inventory.

Answer 2.1

Batches produced and sold	4,000	6,000	9,000
	£	£	£
Sales revenue	140,000	210,000	315,000
Variable costs:			
• Direct materials	22,000	33,000	49,500
• Direct labour	50,000	75,000	112,500
• Overheads	28,000	42,000	63,000
Semi-variable costs:	16,750	22,750	31,750
Total cost	116,750	172,750	256,750
Total profit	23,250	37,250	58,250
Profit per batch (to 2 decimal places)	5.81	6.21	6.47

··

Answer 2.2

(a)

Toy	Elephant	Giraffe
	£	£
Selling price per toy (W1)	2.00	2.00
Less: Unit variable costs		
Direct materials (W2)	0.16	0.20
Direct labour (W3)	0.60	0.50
Variable overheads (W4)	0.04	0.08
Contribution per toy*	1.2	1.22
Profit volume ratio (%)**	60%	61%

* Contribution = Selling price – Variable costs

** Profit volume ratio = Contribution ÷ selling price × 100%

Workings

1   Selling price per bottle

$$\text{Selling price per toy} = \frac{\text{Total sales revenue}}{\text{Sales(toys)}}$$

$$\text{Elephant} = \frac{£2,500}{1,250} = £2 \text{ per toy}$$

$$\text{Giraffe} = \frac{£3,500}{1,750} = £2 \text{ per toy}$$

2   Direct materials per toy

$$\text{Direct materials per toy} = \frac{\text{Total direct labour costs}}{\text{Production volume}}$$

$$\text{Elephant} = \frac{£200}{1,250} = £0.16 \text{ per toy}$$

$$\text{Giraffe} = \frac{£350}{1,750} = £0.20 \text{ per toy}$$

3   Direct labour cost per toy

$$\text{Direct labour cost per toy} = \frac{\text{Total direct labour costs}}{\text{Production volume}}$$

$$\text{Elephant} = \frac{£750}{1,250} = £0.60 \text{ per toy}$$

$$\text{Giraffe} = \frac{£875}{1,750} = £0.50 \text{ per toy}$$

4   Variable overheads per toy

$$\text{Variable overheads per toy} = \frac{\text{Total direct labour costs}}{\text{Production volume}}$$

$$\text{Elephant} = \frac{£50}{1,250} = £0.04 \text{ per toy}$$

$$\text{Giraffe} = \frac{£140}{1,750} = £0.08 \text{ per toy}$$

(b) Breakeven point = Fixed costs/Contribution per unit

= £750/1.22

= 615 units (to the nearest unit)

(c) Margin of safety = Budgeted sales units − breakeven sales units

= 1,750 − 615

= 1,135

Answer 2.3

(a)

	J	K	L	Total
Material requirements				
Kg needed per unit	2	5	3	
Maximum sales demand	50,000	62,500	20,000	
Total kg needed	100,000	312,500	60,000	472,500
Total kg available				490,000

Material shortage NO

	J	K	L	Total
Labour hour requirements				
Labour hours needed per unit	2	4	4	
Maximum sales demand	50,000	62,500	20,000	
Total labour hours needed	100,000	250,000	80,000	430,000
Total labour hours available				400,000

Labour hour shortage YES

227

	J	K	L	Total
Machine hour requirements				
Machine hours needed per unit	4	3	2	
Maximum sales demand	50,000	62,500	20,000	
Total machine hours needed	200,000	187,500	40,000	427,500
Total machine hours available				430,000

Machine hour shortage NO

(b)

	J	K	L
Contribution per unit	37	8	10
Labour hours per unit	2	4	4
Contribution per labour hour	18.5	2	2.5
Ranking	1	3	2

(c)

Product letter	Units	Labour hours used	Cumulative labour hours used
J	50,000	100,000	100,000
L	20,000	80,000	180,000
K	55,000	220,000	400,000

Answer 2.4

	Flexed Budget	Actual	Variance	Favourable (F) or Adverse (A)
Volume sold	410,000	410,000		
	£'000	£'000	£'000	
Sales revenue	12,300	14,350	2,050	F
Less costs:				
Direct materials	2,255	2,460	205	A
Direct labour	1,845	1,640	205	F
Overheads	3,250	4,010	760	A
Operating profit	4,950	6,240	1,290	F

Answer 2.5

(a) The internal rate of return (IRR) is the discount rate that will result in a ⟨ zero ⟩ net present value.

If the IRR of a project is ⟨ higher ⟩ than the organisation's cost of capital then the project should be accepted.

IRR ⟨ does ⟩ take into account the time value of money.

(b) The payback period is **3** years and **4** months.

(c) The project should be accepted.

A net present value is the value of all future cash flows of a project discounted at a particular cost of capital. A positive value indicates the project should be accepted.

BPP PRACTICE ASSESSMENT 5
COSTS AND REVENUES

Time allowed: 2½ hours

Costs and Revenues BPP practice assessment 5

Section 1

Task 1.1

C Ltd uses component GG1 in the production of electric vehicles.

The following inventory record for March 20X1 has been prepared using the FIFO method.

Inventory record card – CG1								
	Receipts			Issues			Balance	
Date	Quantity CG1	Cost per unit (£)	Total cost (£)	Quantity CG1	Cost per unit (£)	Total cost (£)	Quantity CG1	Total cost (£)
4th March							700	10,688
9th March	1,200	16.345	19,614				1,900	30,302
12th March				980	15.268 / 16.345	15,265	920	15,037
17th March	1,200	16.450	19,740				2,120	34,777
31st March				1,100	16.345 / 16.450	17,998	1020	16,779

(a) If C Ltd had adopted the AVCO method what would the final inventory balance on the 9th March have been?

£ [   ]

(Rounded to the nearest £)

(b) If C Ltd had adopted the AVCO method, the value of closing inventory on the 31st March would be [▼]

Picklist

Higher

Lower

The same

(c) The issue of inventory into WIP on the 31st March using the FIFO method would be shown in the accounts as:

Drag and drop the correct account names and type in the value to the nearest £

Drag and drop options:

Materials control account	Work in progress control account
Production control account	Production overhead control account

	Account	(£)
DR		
CR		

Task 1.2

A company had the following transactions during March 20X1:

1.	Spend on production overheads	£3,150
2.	Direct labour (350 hrs)	£3,850
3.	Indirect labour – production salaries	£1,350
4.	Indirect labour – admin salaries	£1,100
5.	Depreciation of factory plant and machinery	£120
6.	Deprecation of office equipment	£50
7.	Production overheads absorbed per direct labour hour	£12.50

(a) **Complete the following journals relating to the production overhead account for March 20X1:**

DR	Production overhead control account	£
CR	Wages and salaries control account	£
DR	Production overhead control account	£
CR	Depreciation account	£
DR	Production overhead control account	£
CR	Bank	£
DR	WIP Account	£
CR	Production overhead control account	£

(b) What is the under or over absorption of overheads during March 20X1?

£ ⬛ | ▼ |

Picklist

Under
Over

....

Task 1.3

Mr Brown is paid based on a combination of hours worked and units produced as follows:

Basic Pay	£8.00 per hour up to 7 hours per day
Overtime	£4.00 per hour premium
Weekend work	£8.00 per hour premium
Production bonus	£0.50 per unit produced per week over 300 units

For week 41, Mr Brown worked 8 hours per day Monday to Friday and 2 hours on Saturday and produced 360 units.

(a) Complete the following payroll record for Mr Brown for week 41.

Provide all values to 2 decimal places

Employee number: 3450		Mr Brown		Week 41
	Hours	Basic pay £	Premium £	Total £
Monday	8			
Tuesday	8			
Wednesday	8			
Thursday	8			
Friday	8			
Saturday	2			
Sunday	-			
Production bonus				
Totals				

(b) The company is considering stopping all premium payments for overtime and instead increasing the production bonus to £0.75 for all units produced each week, over 250 units.

What difference would the difference in pay be for Mr Brown in Week 41 if this policy was adopted?

Provide your answer to 2 decimal places.

£	▼

Picklist

Increase
Decrease

Task 1.4

A Human Resource and Payroll Company has two profit centres/sales departments, HR and Payroll. It also has three service cost centres, Finance, IT and Publications.

The company has the following budgeted overheads for the rest of the year:

	Total (£)	HR (£)	Payroll (£)	Finance (£)	IT (£)	Publications (£)
Rent	62,000					
Building insurance	8,000					
Power, heat & light	19,500					
Printing	61,000					
Software/IT support	39,500					
Salaries	870,000	407,000	168,000	115,000	58,500	121,500

You are also provided with the following information:

	Total	HR	Payroll	Finance	IT	Publications
No. employees	51	22	12	5	3	9
Floor space (sq m)	13,400	5,200	2,700	1,300	1,400	2,800
Publications distributed	18,000	11,000	7,000			

Neither the finance or publications cost centres make use of other cost centres, however all staff make use of the IT department.

(a) **Allocate the overheads to each of the sales and service cost centres on a fair basis showing all values to the nearest £.**

Complete the table below:

Use the drop-down choices to select the basis of apportionment.

	Basis	Total (£)	HR (£)	Payroll (£)	Finance (£)	IT (£)	Publications (£)
Rent	▼	62,000					
Building Insurance	▼	8,000					
Power, heat & light	▼	19,500					
Printing	▼	61,000			-	-	-
Software/IT support	▼	39,000					
Salaries	▼	870,000					
Total		1,059,500					

Picklist

Floor space
Publications distributed
Number of employess

(b) **Reapportion the service centre costs to the sales centres using the step-down approach showing all values to the nearest £.**

Complete the table below:

	Total (£)	HR (£)	Payroll (£)	Finance (£)	IT (£)	Publications (£)
Total	1,059,500					
IT	-				( )	
Total	1,059,500			-		
Finance	-			( )	-	-
Publications	-			-	-	( )
Total				0	0	0

Task 1.5

A company has budgeted and actual levels of production and overheads as follows:

	Budget	Actual
Production (units)	18,000	20,000
Overheads (£)	40,500	41,950
Labour hours (hrs)	9,000	10,200
Machine hours (hrs)	32,400	32,900

(a) What would the overhead absorption rate be if a company based it on direct labour hours? (Answer to 2 decimal places.)

£

(b) What would the overhead absorption rate be if the company based it on machine hours? (Answer to 2 decimal places.)

£

(c) What is the value of overheads absorbed into work-in-progress using (i) direct labour hours (ii) machine hours?

(Show answers to the nearest £)

(i) Overheads absorbed based on direct labour hours	£
(ii) Overheads absorbed based on machine hours	£

(d) What is the value of the under or over absorption of overheads, based on (i) direct labour hours (ii) machine hours?

Use the drop-down box to select whether under or over absorbed.

(i) Based on direct labour hours	▼	£
(ii) Based on machine hours	▼	£

Picklist

Under
Over

(e) Assuming the overheads are absorbed based on machine hours, complete the following journal for overheads:

DR	Production control	£
	Income statement	£
CR	Production overhead control	£

Section 2

Task 2.1

ABC Ltd is in the process of setting production levels for the coming year. The following information is available:

1   Production levels can be either 10,000, 12,000, 14,000 or 16,000 units.

2   All units produced can be sold at a price of £21 per unit.

3   Direct material costs are £6 per unit.

4   Direct labour is £8 per unit up to a production level of 12,000 units. Above this level of production additional supervisors will be required increasing the cost to £9 per unit

5   The machine overheads are semi-variable, dependent on the number of production machines required. The overheads per machine are £11,000. Three machines are required up to a production level of 14,000 units. A fourth machine will be required to produce 16,000 units.

6   General overheads should be calculated using the high-low method. If 10,000 units are produced, the total general overheads will be £18,000. If 16,000 units are produced, the total general overheads will increase to £22,500. (The variable overhead remains constant between these two different production levels.)

(a)   Calculate the profit achieved at each production level and

(b)   state the optimum production level.

(a)   Complete the following table:

	10,000 units	12,000 units	14,000 units	16,000 units
Sales Revenue				
Direct materials				
Direct labour				
Machine overheads				
General overheads				
Total costs				
Profit				

(b)   Optimum production level

Units

Task 2.2

XYZ limited has two KPIs (key performance indicators) which are important in setting price and production levels for product P.

The KPIs are:

    1. To maximise market share achieved by product P

    2. To maximise contribution generated by product P

The demand for product P for the next year at various selling prices is forecast to be:

Sales price (£)	Demand
15	13,000
16	12,500
17	12,000
18	11,000
19	10,000
20	8,000

The production costs for product P for next year are:	
Fixed overheads	£80,000
Direct materials per unit	£3.50
Direct labour per unit	£5.50

XYZ Ltd's strategy is to maximise market share by selling at as low a price as possible. The exact levels of demand are still uncertain so XYZ Ltd has set a break-even volume of 10,000 units.

(a) **If the break-even volume (units) is set at 10,000, what selling price should be set?**

    ☐ £19

    ☐ £17

    ☐ £15

    ☐ £13

(b) **What will be the expected profit earned by XYZ Ltd for product P at this selling price?**

    £ _____

(c) **What is the forecast margin of safety for product P at this selling price? Express your answer as a percentage of XYZ Ltd's break-even volume of 10,000 units.**

(d) **What is the Profit Volume Ratio for XYZ Ltd at the selling price identified in part (a)?**

(Provide you answer to 1 decimal place)

%

Task 2.3

Company X manufactures toys. It has three products it produces and sells: the mouse, the penguin and the elephant.

The production costs for each product are:

	Mouse	Penguin	Elephant
Material A (kg)	0.3	0.5	4.0
Material B (kg)	0.5	0.5	0.5
Labour (hours)	2	3	5

Further information on each of the overheads is as follows:

Costs	
Material A (kg)	£10
Material B (kg)	£26
Labour (per hour)	£12

The selling price and maximum demand at these prices for all three products for the next three months are as follows:

	Mouse	Penguin	Elephant
Sales price (£)	45	70	150
Max demand (£)	400	300	200

(a) **What is the contribution per unit of each product?**

	Mouse	Penguin	Elephant
Contribution (£)			

(b) If the supply of material A is limited to 450kg for the next quarter, what would the maximum total contribution be?

Contribution : £

(c) If the limiting factor was 300kg of Material B, what would the maximum total contribution be?

Contribution: £

(d) What is the optimal production schedule for company X if the supply of both Material A and Material B is sufficient to meet demand, but only 2,750 hours of labour are available during the next quarter?

☐ Produce sufficient of all three products to meet demand

☐ Restrict the production of the mouse

☐ Restrict the production of the penguin

☐ Restrict the production of the elephant

Task 2.4

One Ltd set a budget for December 20X1 based on sales of 6,000 units. However, during the year actual sales were only 5,800 units. The budget together with actual sales and costs is shown below:

	Budget	Actual
Volume sold	6,000	5,800
	£	£
Sales revenue	114,000	109,250
Less costs:		
Material A	33,000	33,450
Material B	21,000	29,150
Direct labour	22,500	20,500
Overheads - Fixed	17,500	17,600
Overheads - Variable	10,500	9,900
Profit	9,500	(1,350)

All materials and direct labour costs are variable costs.

(a) Calculate the flexed budget and the variances between the flexed budget and actual results, for Dec 20X1.

(b) Indicate whether a variance is favourable or adverse using letters F or A.

	Flexed Budget	Actual	Variances	F/A
Volume sold	5,800	5,800		
	£	£	£	
Sales Revenue		109,250		
Material A		33,450		
Material B		29,150		
Direct labour		20,500		
Overheads – fixed		17,600		
Overheads – variable		9,900		
Profit		(1,350)		

(c) What is the primary reason for One Ltd making a loss during December 20X1, when it had originally budgeted to make a profit?

☐ An increase in fixed overheads

☐ Sales being less than budgeted

☐ An increase in time taken to manufacture each unit

☐ An increase in the use and/or the cost of materials

Task 2.5

A company is considering buying new production machinery. The cost and depreciation for the machinery are as follows:

Cost		£150,000
Depreciation	Year 1	£15,000
	Year 2	£15,000
	Year 3	£15,000
Expected sales value	Year 3	£100,000
Expected loss on disposal	Year 3	£5,000

The machinery is forecast to give the following cost savings:

Net cash savings	Year 1	£28,000
	Year 2	£30,000
	Year 3	£32,000

The company appraises projects using a cost of capital of 11%.

PV factors
1.0000
0.9009
0.8116
0.7312

(a) **On the assumption that the company will sell the machinery for the expected value at the end of year 3, what is the net present value (NPV) of the project?**

(Use the – sign to show a negative number)

£

(b) **Should the company accept or reject the opportunity to produce this piece of machinery?**

Picklist

Accept
Reject

(c) **How much of a profit or loss will this piece of machinery contribute to the company over the three years?**

£	▼

Picklist

Profit
Loss

(d) **What is the main reason for the difference between the answers to (b) and (c)?**

☐ The depreciation charged each year is not sufficient to cover the loss on the sale of the machine.

☐ The contribution towards profit does not take into account the time value of money.

☐ The sale proceeds for the machine in three year's time cannot be known with certainty.

☐ The company may be able to buy a second hand machine for less than £150,000.

BPP PRACTICE ASSESSMENT 5
COSTS AND REVENUES

ANSWERS

Costs and Revenues BPP practice assessment 5

Task 1.1

(a) £19,138

Units	Unit cost	Total
700	15.269	10,688
1,200	16.345	19,614
1900		**30,302**

Weighted average cost per unit = 30,302/1,900 = 15.948

Inventory balance   = 1,200 units x 15.948 = £19,138

(b) The answer is (2) - If C Ltd had adopted the AVCO method, the value of closing inventory on the 31st March would be [lower]

Weighted average of balance at 12th March and 17th March

Units		Total
1,200		19,740
920		14,672
2,120		**34,412**

34,412/2,120 = 16.232

Value of inventory at 31st March = 1,020 units x 16.232 = £16,557

(c)

	Account	£
DR	Work in progress control account	17,998
CR	Materials control account	17,998

Task 1.2

(a) Journals relating to the production overhead account for March 20X1:

DR	Production overhead control account	£ 1,350
CR	Wages and salaries control account	£ 1,350
DR	Production overhead control account	£ 120
CR	Depreciation account	£ 120
DR	Production overhead control account	£ 3,150
CR	Bank	£ 3,150
DR	WIP Account (350 x 12.50)	£ 4,375
CR	Production overhead control account	£ 4,375

(b) Under absorption of overheads during March 20X1

$(1350 + 120 + 3150) - 4375 = 245$

£ 245		Under

....

Task 1.3

(a)

Employee number: 3450		Mr Brown		Week 41
	Hours	Basic pay (£)	Premium (£)	Total (£)
Monday	8	64.00	4.00	68.00
Tuesday	8	64.00	4.00	68.00
Wednesday	8	64.00	4.00	68.00
Thursday	8	64.00	4.00	68.00
Friday	8	64.00	4.00	68.00
Saturday	2	16.00	16.00	32.00
Sunday	-	-		
Production bonus		30.00		30.00
Total		366.00	36.00	402.00

BPP LEARNING MEDIA

(b)

	£
Production bonus £0.75 x 110	82.50
Less original premium	(66.00)
Increase in pay	16.50

Task 1.4

(a)

	Basis	Total (£)	HR (£)	Payroll (£)	Finance (£)	IT (£)	Publications (£)
Rent	Floor space	62,000	24,060	12,493	6,015	6,478	12,954
Building Insurance	Floor space	8,000	3,104	1,612	776	836	1,672
Power, heat & light	Floor space	19,500	7,567	3,929	1,892	2,037	4,075
Printing	Publications distributed	61,000	37,278	23,772	-	-	-
Software/IT support	No. employees	39,000	16,824	9,176	3,824	2,294	6,882
Salaries	No. employees	870,000	407,000	168,000	115,000	58,500	121,500
Total		1,059,500	495,833	218,932	127,507	70,145	147,083

(b)

	Total (£)	HR (£)	Payroll (£)	Finance (£)	IT (£)	Publicat-ions (£)
Total	1,059,500	495,833	218,932	127,507	70,145	147,083
IT	-	32,150	17,536	7,307	(70,145)	13,152
Total	1,059,500	527,983	236,468	134,814	-	160,235
Finance	-	87,234	47,580	(134,814)	-	-
Publications	-	103,681	56,554	-	-	(160,235)
Total				0	0	0

Notes for both (a) and (b) above:

- Rent, building insurance, power, heat and light are apportioned on the basis of floor space: 52:27:13:14:28

- Printing costs are apportioned on the basis of publication distributed 7:11

- Software and IT support costs are apportioned on the basis of number of employees 22:12:5:3:9

- Costs from the IT cost centre are apportioned to all departments on the basis of number of employees 22:12:5:9

- Costs from the finance and publications cost centres are apportioned on the basis of number of employees 22:12

Task 1.5

(a)

£ 4.50

(b)

£ 1.25

(c)

(i) Overheads absorbed based on direct labour hours	£ 45,900
(ii) Overheads absorbed based on machine hours	£ 41,125

(d)

(i) Based on direct labour hours	Over	£ 3,950
(ii) Based on machine hours	Under	£ 825

(e)

DR	Production control	£41,125
	Income statement	£825
CR	Production overhead control	£41,950

Section 2

Task 2.1

(a)

	10,000 units	12,000 units	14,000 units	16,000 units
Sales Revenue	210,000	252,000	294,000	336,000
Direct materials	60,000	72,000	84,000	96,000
Direct labour	80,000	96,000	126,000	144,000
Machine overheads	33,000	33,000	33,000	44,000
General overheads	18,000	19,500	21,000	22,500
Total costs	191,000	220,500	264,000	306,500
Profit	19,000	31,500	30,000	29,500

(b) Optimum production level

12,000   Units

....

Task 2.2

(a) The correct answer is £17

Sales price (£)	Contribution (£)	Break-even units
15	6	13,333
16	7	11,429
17	**8**	**10,000**
18	9	8,889
19	10	8,000
20	11	7,272

(b) The expected profit earned

	£
Sales (£17 x 12,000)	204,000
Direct materials (£3.50 x 12,000)	(42,000)
Direct labour (£5.50 x 12,000)	(66,000)
Fixed overheads	(80,000)
Profit	16,000

(c) Working (2,000/10,000) x 100 = 20%

(d) Contribution/sales = (£8/£17) x 100 = 47.1%

Task 2.3

(a) Contribution per unit of each product:

	Mouse	Penguin	Elephant
Sales price	45	70	150
Material A	(3)	(5)	(40)
Material B	(13)	(13)	(13)
Labour	(24)	(36)	(60)
Contribution (£)	**5**	**16**	**37**

(b) If the limiting factor was Material A (450kg) the maximum total contribution would be:

	Mouse	Penguin	Elephant
Contribution (£)	5	16	37
Use Material A (kg)	0.3	0.5	4.00
Contribution per kg (£)	16.67	32	9.25
Ranking	2	1	3
Total requirement of Material A	120	150	800
Use of Material A	120	150	180
Production level	400	300	45
Total contribution	2,000	4,800	1,665

Contribution : £8,465

(c) **If the limiting factor was Material B (300kg) the maximum total contribution would be:**

	Mouse	Penguin	Elephant
Contribution (£)	5	16	37
Use material B (kg)	0.5	0.5	0.5
Contribution per kg (£)	10	32	74
Ranking	3	2	1
Total requirement of Material B	200	150	100
Use of Material B	50	150	100
Production level	100	300	200
Total contribution	500	4,800	7,400

Contribution: £ 12,700

(d) The optimal production schedule for company X if the supply of both Material A and Material B is sufficient to meet demand:

Produce sufficient of all three products to meet demand

		Mouse	Penguin	Elephant
Labour hours per unit		2	3	5
Demand		400	300	200
Maximum labour hours required		800	900	1,000
Total	2,700	Not a limiting factor		

Task 2.4

(a)+(b)

	Flexed Budget	Actual	Variances	F/A
Volume sold	5,800	5,800		
	£	£	£	
Sales Revenue	110,200	109,250	950	A
Material A	31,900	33,450	1,550	A
Material B	20,300	29,150	8,850	A
Direct labour	21,750	20,500	1,250	F
Overheads – fixed	17,500	17,600	100	A
Overheads – variable	10,150	9,900	250	F
Profit	8,600	(1,350)	9,950	A

(c) The answer is An increase in the use and/or the cost of materials

Task 2.5

(a) The net present value (NPV) of the project:

Time	Cash costs	Cash inflows	Net cash flows	PV factors	Discounted cash flows
0	(150,000)		(150,000)	1.0000	(150,000)
1		28,000	28,000	0.9009	25,225
2		30,000	30,000	0.8116	24,348
3		132,000	132,000	0.7312	96,518
			Net present value		(3,909)

NPV £-3,909

(b) Should the company accept or reject the opportunity to produce this piece of machinery?

Reject

(c) The profit is calculated:

Year 1	28,000 – 15,000 (savings less depreciation)	£13,000
Year 2	30,000 – 15,000 (savings less depreciation)	£15,000
Year 3	32,000 – 15,000 – 5,000 (savings less depreciation less loss on disposal)	£12,000
Total		£40,000

£ 40,000	Profit

(d) The correct answer is The contribution towards profit does not take into account the time value of money.

BPP PRACTICE ASSESSMENT 6
COSTS AND REVENUES

Time allowed: 2½ hours

Costs and Revenues BPP practice assessment 6

Section 1

Task 1.1

NMC Ltd manufactures bricks for the housing sector. At present the Economic Order Quantity for raw material A is 2,500 containers of bricks. This is based on the following levels of demand and costs.

Annual demand: 40,000 containers

Annual holding cost per container: £32

Order cost: £2,500 (fixed for an annual demand of 40,000 and above)

As a result of changes in general economic conditions and the introduction of a new warehousing facility at NMC, the production and finance managers are currently reassessing demand and inventory management.

The following information is available:

- The new warehousing facility will reduce holding costs by 10%

- Due to poor performances in the housing market and a fall in new builds, demand is estimated to have fallen by 20%

- Order costs remain constant. However, for an annual demand below 40,000 a 10% premium will be payable

(a) Calculate the new Economic Order Quantity for material A. Provide your answer to the nearest whole container.

containers

(b) NMC records all receipts and issues of material in the new integrated accounts system.

The following information is available:

(1) On 1st March 20X1 2,500 containers of material A were received by NMC from the supplier on credit.

(2) On 5th March 20X1 700 containers were issued to production.

(3) On 5th March 20X1 20 containers were identified as sub-standard and returned to the supplier.

Use the drag and drop options below to show the cost accounting treatment for each of these transactions:

Drag and drop options:

Inventory	Bank	Finished Goods	Trade Receivables	Inventory
Trade Receivables	Trade Payables	Production	Bank	Trade Payables

Cost accounting treatment				
(1)	DR		CR	
(2)	DR		CR	
(3)	DR		CR	

(c) On 31st March 20X1 NMC started using the new Economic Order Quantity for material A.

Complete the inventory record below using the AVCO method of issuing and valuing inventory:

Assume receipts are equal to the EOQ.

Show all quantities and totals as whole numbers and unit costs to 3 decimal places.

	Receipts			Issues			Balance	
Date	Quantity (container)	Cost per container (£)	Total cost (£)	Quantity (containers)	Cost per unit (£)	Total cost (£)	Quantity (containers)	Total cost (£)
Balance at 31 March							250	162,500
9th April			98,000	785				
12th April				450				

··

Task 1.2

PBB Ltd has budgeted sales of 15,000 units per month in Quarter 3 of 20X1. It sells each unit for £35.00 and direct costs per unit are £7.50. Budgeted overheads per month are £16,000.

Overheads are absorbed into production on a machine hour basis. Each unit requires 2 ½ machine hours and 1½ labour hours.

(a) Calculate the budgeted machine hours and the overheads absorption rate based on the information above.

Budgeted machine hours		hrs
OAR based on machine hours (2dp)	£	per machine hour

(b) The following actual overheads were incurred:

July	£17,500
August	£14,000
September	£16,250

Assuming all other costs and activities remain constant calculate the over/under absorption and show the accounting treatment for overheads in July and August.

Complete the table below:

Under/over absorption:

July	Under/Over absorbed	£
August	Under/Over absorbed	£

Accounting treatment:

Drag and drop the options to show the accounting treatment for the under/over absorption of overheads in July and August.

Drag and drop options:

Income statement	Production overhead control
Income statement	Production overhead control

July	DR		CR	
August	DR		CR	

(c) In September production and sales only reached 13,000 units.

Calculate:

(i) **The actual machine hours used in September**

Machine hours

(ii) **The under/over absorption of overheads in September, and state whether they were under or over absorbed**

Under/Over absorbed   £ _____

(iii) **The actual profit for September taking account of any under/over absorption**

£ _____

Task 1.3

BYC Ltd is a busy tele-sales and internet sales company based in Europe. Employees at BYC work 40 core hours per week based on 8 hours per day. Payment for core hours, overtime and bonuses are as follows:

- Core hours are paid at £10.60 per hour

- A premium of half the hourly rate is paid for weekday overtime

- A premium of the full hourly rate is paid for weekend overtime

- Any calls/requests handled beyond 500 in any one week will attract a bonus per call/request of £0.30

- An additional weekly bonus will be paid if a worker handles more than 1,000 calls in any one week. This bonus is £1,000.

The hours worked and calls/requests handled for one employee, Bill Raynet, for week 29 were as follows:

Bill Raynet	Employee number:567	Week 29
	Hours worked	Calls/requests handled
Monday	9	130
Tuesday	8	126
Wednesday	10	234
Thursday	8	167
Friday	9	245
Saturday	3	134
Sunday	2	230

Using the information provided:

(a) **Calculate the total pay for Bill Raynet in week 29 (to 2 decimal places).**

£ _____

(b) **How much of Bill's pay will be allocated to indirect labour costs?**

(State your answer to the nearest whole £.)

£ _____

(c) **If the one off bonus of £1,000 was scrapped and replaced by an overall increase in the core hourly rate of 5%, what would Bill's total pay be for week 29? (to 2 decimal places).**

£ _____

(d) **With the increase in the core pay of 5%, how much of Bill's pay will be allocated to direct labour costs in week 29? (State your answer to the nearest whole £)**

£ _____

Task 1.4

LSB Ltd has prepared the budgeted overhead apportionment and re-apportionment shown below using the direct method.

The maintenance department uses the services of the stores, and as a result the finance director is considering changing to the step down method.

Part 1: You have been asked to prepare a comparison for the finance director to review.

The following information is available:

- General Admin costs are split 50:50
- There are no reciprocal services to or from General Admin.

Budgeted use of service centres:

	Brushing	Sleeking	Maintenance
Materials requisitions	25	15	6
Maintenance hours	300	100	-

	Basis of apportion ment	Totals £	Brushing £	Sleeking £	Maintenance £	Stores £	General Admin £
Depreciation of plant and equipment	NBV of Plant and equipment	650,000	450,000	200,000			
Power for production machinery	Production machinery power usage (KwH)	560,900	388,315	172,585			
Rent and rates	Floor space	97,000			43,650	29,100	24,250
Light and heat	Floor space	34,000			15,300	10,200	8,500
Indirect labour	Allocated	238,350			124,500	34,950	78,900
Totals		1,580,250	838,315	372,585	183,450	74,250	111,650
Reapportion Maintenance			108,236	75,214	(143,480)		
Reapportion Stores			29,700	44,550		(94,520)	
Reapportion General Admin			55,825	55,825			(297,310
Total overheads to production centres		1,580,250	1,032,076	548,174			

(a) Re-apportion overheads using the step down approach.

Complete the table below:

	Totals £	Brushing £	Sleeking £	Maintenance £	Stores £	General Admin £
	1,580,250	838,315	372,585	183,450	74,250	111,650
Reapportion Maintenance/Stores						
Reapportion Maintenance/Stores						
Reapportion General Admin						
Total overheads to production centres	1,580,250					

Part 2: You have also been asked to calculate the overhead absorption rate for the two departments using the totals from the step down approach.

(a) Select the most appropriate basis on which to absorb overheads for each department.

Tick your chosen basis:

Brushing	Labour hours		Machine hours	
Sleeking	Labour hours		Machine hours	

(b) Using the basis you selected above calculate the budgeted overhead absorption rate for each department.

The following additional information is provided:

	Brushing	Sleeking
Budgeted direct labour hours	1.75 hrs per unit	3 hrs per unit
Total hours	1,750 hrs	3,000 hrs
Budgeted machine hours	2.5 hrs	1 hr
Total hours	2,500 hrs	1,000 hrs

Insert your answer below (to 2 decimal places):

Brushing	£	Machine/Labour hour
Sleeking	£	Machine/Labour hour

Task 1.5

Glide Ltd produces snowboards for worldwide distribution at a selling price of £300 per board. The company has two production departments, moulding and packaging. The budgeted production for June 20X1 is 15,000 boards. Overheads are absorbed on a direct labour hours basis.

The following information is provided:

Budgeted costs:	
Direct materials	£25 per unit
Direct labour:	
Moulding	4 hours per board at £9.00 per hour
Packaging	1 hour per board at £7.50 per hour

Variable overheads:	
Moulding	£230,000
Packaging	£120,000

Fixed overheads:	
Moulding	£150,000
Packaging	£80,000

(a) **Calculate the cost per unit using absorption costing (to two decimal places).**

£

(b) **Calculate the prime cost using marginal costing (to two decimal places).**

£

The actual production and sales for May and June 20X1 were as follows:

	May	June
Sales	14,000	13,000
Production	14,000	15,000

(c) Calculate the profit for June under each of the two costing methods, and the difference between each.

Complete the table below:

	£'000
Absorption costing profit	
Marginal costing profit	
Difference	

Section 2

Task 2.1

C & M Ltd is a cleaning and maintenance company. One of C & M Ltd's customers is 9 to 5 Ltd, and this company has already awarded C & M Ltd the contract to clean and maintain Office A.

C & M Ltd charges customers a fixed weekly rate based on the contracted number of hours work. The contract for Office A is for 100 hours per week and will require four employees to carry out the work.

C & M Ltd's cost and profit profile for Office A is:

Cost Type	Rate	Weekly Cost £
Direct labour	£8 per hour	800
Direct materials	£10 per hour	1,000
Transport	£50 per employee	200
Supervisor's wages	£100 per contract	100
General overheads	Fixed weekly amount	500
Total costs		2,600
Profit element	£9 per hour	900
Contract price	£35 per hour	3,500

9 to 5 Ltd has asked C & M Ltd to quote for the contracts on two more buildings, Office B and Office C.

Office B will require 150 hours labour per week, and because the time available to carry out the work each day is restricted, C & M Ltd will need to allocate 8 employees to the contract.

Office C will require 175 hours labour each week, and will need 6 employees.

9 to 5 Ltd has asked C & M Ltd to give them a discount on the current price of £35 per hour if they award the contracts for all three offices to C & M Ltd.

(a) **C & M Ltd wish to continue making a profit of at least £9 per hour. What contract price would C & M Ltd need to charge for Offices B and C in order to cover all their costs and still make this level of profit? What would be the total contract price for all three offices at this level of profit?**

Contract price for Office B £ ⬚

Contract price for Office C £ ⬚

Contract price for all three offices £ ⬚

(b) **What is the total contract price for all three offices that C & M Ltd would charge at the current contact price of £35 per hour? What percentage discount can they give on this price (to 1 decimal place) in order to still achieve a profit of £9 per hour?**

Contract price for all 3 offices at £35 per hour £ ⬚

Maximum discount ⬚ %

Task 2.2

A company achieved the following profit levels at each of the two given sales levels:

Units sold	Profit (£)
200	15,000
300	35,000

The selling price is fixed, and all costs are either fixed or variable (there are no stepped costs).

(a) **What is the contribution per unit?**

Contribution per unit £ ⬚

(b) **What are the fixed costs?**

Fixed costs £ ⬚

(c) **What is the break-even point?**

Break-even point ⬚ units

Task 2.3

A manufacturing company passes raw materials and work in progress through three separate production processes. These are called Processes 1, 2 and 3.

During the quarter ended 31 December 20X0, 200kg of output with a value of £74,200 was passed from Process 1 to Process 2. Process 2 normally expects to suffer a loss of 10%, but during this quarter it suffered a loss of only 9%. The waste can be sold for scrap at £15 per kg.

During the quarter ended 31 December 20X0, the following labour and overhead costs were allocated to Process 2.

Labour £18,750

Overheads £14,270

(a) **You are required to complete the following process account for Process 2 for the quarter ended 31 December 20X0:**

Description	Kg	£		Description	Kg	£
Input from Process 1				Normal loss		
Labour				Output		
Overheads						
Abnormal gain						
Total				Total		

(b) **What is the value of the abnormal loss from Process 2 that will be credited to the income statement?**

Credit to income statement   £

....

Task 2.4

A local authority sells advertising space on a number of advertising hoardings in its area. The monthly budgeted contribution per hoarding generated from these sales is as follows:

Sales	£350
Variable costs	£260
Contribution	£90

Fixed costs allocated to the advertising department are budgeted at £2,000 per month.

The monthly budget is based on sales of 75 advertising spaces. However during the first two months of 20X1 the actual sales achieved were:

Month	Sales (units)	Sales £	Variable costs £	Fixed costs £
January 20X1	67	20,800	17,700	1,980
February 20X1	79	28,520	20,190	2,390

You are required to complete the following tables in order to calculate the monthly variances between the actual results and the flexed budget, showing whether each variance is favourable (F) or adverse (A).

January 20X1	Actual results	Monthly budget	Flexed budget	Variance	Favourable (F) or Adverse (A)
Sales Volume					
	£	£	£	£	£
Sales					
Variable costs					
Fixed costs					
Profit					

February 20X1	Actual results	Monthly budget	Flexed budget	Variance	Favourable (F) or Adverse (A)
Sales Volume					
	£	£	£	£	£
Sales					
Variable costs					
Fixed costs					
Profit					

Task 2.5

A Ltd has forecast the following accounting entries for the next four years, which relate to the proposed purchase of a new production line:

Year ending 31 December 20X5	
Purchase of plant and machinery on 1 January 20X5	£615,000
Depreciation charge for year	£41,000
Savings in production costs	£220,000
Year ending 31 December 20X6	
Depreciation charge for year	£41,000
Savings in production costs	£220,000
Year ending 31 December 20X5	
Repairs to production line	£25,000
Year ending 31 December 20X7	
Depreciation charge for year	£41,000
Savings in production costs	£220,000
Repairs to production line	£40,000
Year ending 31 December 20X8	
Depreciation charge for year	£41,000
Savings in production costs	£220,000
Repairs to production line	£60,000

The company appraises projects using a 10% cost of capital.

(a) You are required to calculate the Net Present Value of the proposed purchase of the new production line by completing the following table:

Time	Net Cash Flows £	Discount Factor at 10%	Discounted Cash Flows £
T0		1.0000	
T1		0.9091	
T2		0.8264	
T3		0.7513	
T4		0.6830	
Net Present Value			

(b) State whether the company should accept or reject the proposal.

Accept / Reject

(c) If A Ltd increases the cost of capital that it uses to appraise projects to 12%, will this increase or decrease the net present value of this project, or have no effect?

Increase / Decrease / No Effect

BPP PRACTICE ASSESSMENT 6
COSTS AND REVENUES

ANSWERS

Answer bank

Task 1.1

(a)

$$EOQ = \sqrt{\frac{2cd}{h}}$$

h is reduced by 10% = £28.80

d is reduced by 20% = 32,000 $\sqrt{\frac{2 \times 2,750 \times 32,000}{28.80}}$

c is increased by 10% as the demand falls below 40,000 = £2,750

New EOQ = $\sqrt{\frac{2 \times 2,750 \times 32,000}{28.80}}$ = 2,472 containers

to the nearest whole container is

> **2,472 containers**

(b)

(1)	DR	Inventory		CR	Trade Payables
(2)	DR	Production		CR	Inventory
(3)	DR	Trade Payables		CR	Inventory

(c)

	Receipts			Issues			Balance	
Date	Quantity (containers	Cost per container (£)	Total cost (£)	Quantity (containers)	Cost per unit (£)	Total cost (£)	Quantity (containers)	Total cost (£)
Balance as at 31 March							250	11,100
9th April	2,472	39.644	98,000	785	40.081 (W1)	31,464	1,937	77,637
12th April				450	40.081	1,8036	1,487	59,600

Working 1:

250 containers	£11,100
2,472 containers	£98,000
2,722	£109,100
109,100/2,722 = **40.081**	

Task 1.2

(a)

Budgeted machine hours 15,000 x 2.5	**37,500 hrs**
OAR based on machine hours = Overheads/machine hours = 16,000/37,500	**£0.43 per machine hour**

(b)

Under/over absorption:

July Actual = 17,500 Budget = 16,000	**Under absorbed**	**£ 1,500**
August Actual = 14,000 Budget = 16,000	**Over absorbed**	**£ 2,000**

Accounting treatment:

July	DR	Income statement	CR	Production overhead control
August	DR	Production overhead control	CR	Income statement

(c)

(i) The actual machine hours used in September

(13,000 x 2.5)

32,500 machine hours

(ii) The under/over absorption of overheads in September

Actual production	13,000 units	= 32,500 hours
Actual overhead absorbed	32,500 x 0.43	=£13,975
Actual overhead		£16,250
Difference	£16,250 - £13,975	= £2,275

£ 2,275

Under absorbed

(iii) The actual profit for September taking account of any under/over absorption

£ 339,225

Sales 13,000 x £35.00	455,000
Less:	
Direct costs	(97,500)
Overheads	(16,000)
LESS: Under absorption	(2,275)
Profit	**339,225**

Task 1.3

	Hours worked	Calls/requests handled	Pay at core rate	Overtime hrs	Premium £	Total £
Monday	9	130	95.40	1	5.30	100.70
Tuesday	8	128	84.80	0	0.00	84.80
Wednesday	10	234	106.00	2	10.60	116.60
Thursday	8	167	84.80	0	0.00	84.80
Friday	9	245	95.40	1	5.30	100.70
Saturday	3	134	31.80	3	31.80	63.60
Sunday	2	230	21.20	2	21.20	42.40
Total	49	1268	519.40		74.20	593.60

Requests handled over 500	768
Bonus payment	**230.40**

Bonus payment for over 1,000 calls/requests			£1,000

(a) **Total pay** for Bill in week 29

Total pay (593.60) + Bonus over 500 (229.80) +Bonus over 1,000 (1,000)

£1,823.40

(b) Pay allocated to **indirect labour** costs

Bonus + premium payments = 230.40 + 1,000 + 74.20

£1,305

(c) Bill's **total pay** for week 29 if the £1,000 bonus was scrapped:

£853.66

Core rate = 11.13 (10.60 x 1.05)

	Hours worked	Calls/requests handled	Pay at core rate	Overtime	Premium	Total
Monday	9	130	100.17	1	5.56	105.73
Tuesday	8	128	89.04	0	0.00	89.04
Wednesday	10	234	111.30	2	11.12	122.42
Thursday	8	167	89.04	0	0.00	89.04
Friday	9	245	100.17	1	5.56	105.73
Saturday	3	134	33.39	3	33.39	66.78
Sunday	2	230	22.26	2	22.26	44.52
Total	49	1268	545.37		77.89	**623.26**

Requests handles over 500	
	768
Payment	**230.40**

Total pay = 623.26 + 230.40 = £853.66

(d) Pay allocated to **<u>direct labour</u>** costs in week 29 if the £1,000 bonus was scrapped:

£545

Task 1.4

Part 1: (a) Re-apportion – step down method:

Totals	Totals £	Brushing £	Sleeking £	Maintenance £	Stores £	General Admin £
	1,580,250	838,315	372,585	183,450	74,250	111,650
Reapportion Stores		41,250	24,750	8,250	(74,250)	
		879,565	397,335	191,700		111,650
Reapportion Maintenance		47,925	143,775	(191,700)		
		927,490	541,110			111,650
Reapportion General Admin		55,825	55,825			(111,650)
Total overheads to production centres	1,580,250	983,315	596,935			

Part 2:

(a) The most appropriate basis:

Brushing	Machine hours	√
Sleeking	Labour hours	√

(b) The budgeted overhead absorption rate for each department.

Brushing	983,315/2,500 = £393.33 per machine hour
Sleeking	596,935/3,000 = £198.98 per labour hour

Task 1.5

(a) The cost per unit using **absorption costing**:

		Moulding	Packaging
Total overheads		£380,000	£200,000
Total labour hours	15,000 x 4	60,000	
	15,000 x 1		15,000
OAR		380,000/60,000=**6.33**	200,000/15,000=**13.33**

Direct Materials			25.00
	Direct labour	Moulding	36.00
		Packaging	7.50
	Overheads	Moulding (6.33 x4)	25.32
		Packaging (13.33 x 1)	13.33
Total unit cost			**£107.15**

(b) The cost per unit using **marginal costing**:

		Moulding	Packaging
Variable overheads		£230,000	£120,000
Total labour hours	15,000 x 4	60,000	
	15,000 x 1		15,000
OAR		230,000/60,000=**3.83**	120,000/15,000=**8.00**

Direct Materials			25.00
	Direct labour	Moulding	36.00
		Packaging	7.50
	Overheads	Moulding (3.83 x4)	15.32
		Packaging (8.00 x 1)	8.00
Prime cost			**£91.82**

(c)   Absorption cost profit:

	£	£
Sales (13,000 x 300)		3,900,000
Less: cost of sales		
Opening inventory	-	
Cost of production (15,000 x 107.15)	1,607,250	
Less closing inventory	-214,300	1,392,950
Profit		2,507,050

Marginal costing profit:

	£	£
Sales		3,900,000
Less: cost of sales		
Opening inventory	-	
Cost of production (15,000 x 91.82)	1,377,300	
Less closing inventory	-183,640	
		1,193,660
Contribution		2,706,340
Less fixed costs		230,000
Profit		2,476,340

	£'000
Absorption costing profit	2,507
Marginal costing profit	2,476
Difference	31

Section 2

Task 2.1

(a)

Cost Type	Rate	Office A (£)	Office B (£)	Office C (£)
Number of hours		100	150	175
Number of employees		4	8	6
Direct labour	£8 per hour	800	1,200	1,400
Direct materials	£10 per hour	1,000	1,500	1,750
Transport	£50 per employee	200	400	300
Supervisor's wages	£100 per contract	100	100	100
General overheads	Fixed weekly amount per contract	500	500	500
Total costs		2,600	3,700	4,050
Required profit	£9 per hour	900	1,350	1,575
Minimum contract price		3,500	5,050	5,625

Contract price for Office B — £5,050

Contract price for Office C — £5,625

Contract price for all 3 offices — £14,175

(b)

Total number of hours (all three offices)	425
Standard contract price (£35 ph)	£14,875
Minimum contract price at profit of £9 ph	£14,175
Discount to be offered (£)	£700
Discount to be offered (%)	4.7%

Contract price for all 3 offices at £35 per hour — £14,875

Maximum discount — 4.7%

Task 2.2

(a)

Units sold	Profit (£)
200	15,000
300	35,000
Difference = 100 units	20,000
Contribution per unit	200

Contribution per unit   £200

(b)

Sales level of 200 units	£
Contribution (£200 per unit)	40,000
Profit	15,000
Difference fixed costs	25,000

Fixed costs   £25,000

(c) Break-even point = fixed costs / contribution per unit

   = £25,000 / £200

   = 125 units

Break-even point   125 units

....

Task 2.3

(a)

Description	Kg	£	Description	Kg	£
Input from Process 1	200	74,200	Normal loss	20	300
Labour		18,750	Output	182	108,108
Overheads		14,270			
Abnormal gain	2	1,188			
Total	202	108,408	Total	202	108,408

Workings

Expected output	= 200kg – 20kg= 180kg
Actual output	= 200kg – 18kg= 182kg
Value of normal loss	= 20kg x £15= £300
Process costs	= £74,200 + £18,750 +£14,270 – £300= £106,920
Value of expected output	= £106,920 / 180kg= £594 per kg
Value of actual output	= 182kg x £594= £108,108
Value of abnormal gain	= 2kg x £594= £1,188

(b) Credit to income statement

£1,218

Workings

Credit from Process 2 = £1,188

Scrap proceeds = 2kg x £15 = £30

Total credit to income statement = £1,218

Task 2.4

January 20X1					
	Actual results	Monthly budget	Flexed budget	Variance	Favourable (F) or Adverse (A)
Sales Volume	67	75	67		
	£	£	£	£	£
Sales	20,800	26,250	23,450	2,650	A
Variable costs	17,700	19,500	17,420	280	A
Fixed costs	1,980	2,000	2,000	20	F
Profit	1,120	4,750	4,030	2,910	A

February 20X1	Actual results	Monthly budget	Flexed budget	Variance	Favourable (F) or Adverse (A)
Sales Volume	79	75	79		
	£	£	£	£	£
Sales	28,520	26,250	27,650	870	F
Variable costs	20,190	19,500	20,540	350	F
Fixed costs	2,390	2,000	2,000	390	A
Profit	5,940	4,750	5,110	830	F

Task 2.5

(a)

Time	Net Cash Flows £	Discount Factor at 10%	Discounted Cash Flows £
T0	(615,000)	1.0000	(615,000)
T1	220,000	0.9091	200,002
T2	195,000	0.8264	161,148
T3	180,000	0.7513	135,234
T4	160,000	0.6830	109,280
Net Present Value			(9,336)

(b) **Accept / Reject**   Reject

(c) **Increase / Decrease / No Effect**   Decrease

Notes

Notes